Myron S. Augsburger, President Emeritus of the Coalition of Christian Colleges and Universities

The Grace Connection is for the honest person who dares not only to think *about* God but to think *with* God. The glory of humanity is that we can pray, and we can open our lives to the mystery of God. James Fairfield treats prayer as the heartbeat of a nontraditional disciple. This work is an intriguing call to solidarity with Christ. It is a book to be enjoyed, one that will engage us where faith meets life.

Philip L. Dougherty †, CFX, Theological Consultant, Catholic Diocese of Richmond

"In God we live and have our being," Paul of Tarsus advised the citizens of Athens nearly two millennia ago. In *The Grace Connection*, James Fairfield shares some of what he has experienced and learned about prayer and living, moving and being in God. I recommend this easy-to-read, highly personal account of a contemporary believer's encounter with God in prayer.

John M. Drescher, Pastor, Author of more than thirty-five books and articles in more than a hundred periodicals

This is a refreshing and rewarding look at the prayer Jesus taught the disciples to pray. There is no doubt in James Fairfield's mind that God is here and his reign is present. God is relevant in our experience now, right where we are. I was intrigued, inspired, and stimulated in this study and the stories woven so meaningfully into the pattern of the most prayed prayer of the Christian church.

FINDING GOD'S FAVOR
─── 1 ───

The Grace Connection

Spiritual Power from the Lord's Prayer

James G. T. Fairfield

Herald
Press

HERALD PRESS
Scottdale, Pennsylvania
Waterloo, Ontario

Library of Congress Cataloging-in-Publication Data
Fairfield, James G. T., 1926-
　　The grace connection : spiritual power from the Lord's Prayer / James G. T. Fairfield.
　　　p.　　cm. — (Finding God's favor ; 1)
　　Includes bibliographical references.
　　ISBN 0-8361-9091-2 (alk. paper)
　　1. Spiritual life—Christianity. 2. Lord's prayer. I. Title.
II. Series: Fairfield, James G. T., 1926-　Finding God's favor ; 1.
BV4501.2.F285　1998 vol. 1
[BV230]
226.9'606—DC21　　　　　　　　　　　　　　　　　　　　　98-23542

The paper used in this publication is recycled and meets the minimum requirements of the American National Standard for Information Sciences—Permanence of Paper for Printed Library Materials, ANSI Z39.48-1984.

Scripture is used by permission, all rights reserved, and is usually from *Holy Bible, New International Version* ®, copyright © 1973, 1978, 1984 by International Bible Society, Zondervan Publishing House. NRSV, from the New Revised Standard Version Bible, copyright 1989, by the Division of Christian Education of the National Council of the Churches of Christ in the USA. Some texts are adapted from KJV, *The King James Version of the Bible*.

THE GRACE CONNECTION
Copyright © 1998 by Herald Press, Scottdale, Pa. 15683
　　Published simultaneously in Canada by Herald Press,
　　Waterloo, Ont. N2L 6H7. All rights reserved
Library of Congress Catalog Card Number: 98-23542
International Standard Book Number: 0-8361-9091-2
Printed in the United States of America
Book and cover design and art by Merrill R. Miller

07 06 05 04 03 02 01 00 99 98 10 9 8 7 6 5 4 3 2 1

*To Norma,
who has always tried to be her own person
in relation to God
so that her faith can be focused and true.*

Contents

Foreword by David Augsburger 7
Preface 11
How to Use This Book 13

1. Why Pray? 15
2. Our Father 27
3. Who art in heaven 37
4. Hallowed be thy name 47
5. Thy kingdom come 57
6. Thy will be done 67
7. On earth as it is in heaven 77
8. Give us this day our daily bread 87
9. Forgive us our trespasses 97
10. As we forgive those who trespass against us 107
11. Lead us not into temptation,
    but deliver us from evil 117
12. For thine is the kingdom, the power,
    and the glory, forever and ever. Amen 127

Study Guide and Notes 137
Bibliography 141
The Author 143

Foreword

The most familiar, the most common, the prayer we know best—the disciples' prayer misnamed "The Lord's Prayer"—is a great mystery.

How shall we understand it? Dare we pray it? Who of us can live it? It is the prayer that unites us to all other believers, yet reveals our individual failings. It is collective yet personal, communal yet individual.

You are about to enter a book that seeks to illuminate the mysterious intrigue we sense yet largely miss as we repeat the well-known and much loved. As we pray it, we love it, know it, understand it, yet find it much beyond our grasp. To point out the hidden outlines of this fascinating enigma hidden within these most-memorized and most-automatically repeatable words, here is an opening sketch of a few clues, of several visible and unmistakable signs of the tremendous, of the mysterious.

Mystery one: the plural language. The prayer is set in the language of a circle of believers around Jesus. Its words are "*our* Father . . . give *us* . . . *our* daily bread . . . lead *us* . . . deliver *us*. . . ." It is a community prayer. No one can pray it alone. The first word places the speaker in community whether uttered in a group or whispered alone. Even if no one else is present at the moment of prayer, all fellow believers are summoned into the circle of faith from the first syllable.

Mystery two: the direction. "Our Father in heaven." Heaven is not a concrete place, no divine Bermuda or Hawaii.

It is a seventh dimension beyond our empirical maps of latitude, longitude, altitude, time, being, speed of light, and still unnamed dimensions. It is a spiritual reality outside of our sensory, theoretical, or conceptual realities. More than a place it is the source, the ground, the home of all created places. And it is there, as God whom we address is there.

Mystery three: the name. The name of the Father is unpronounceable; it is the unspeakable, not to be uttered. No one knows its sounds, only the initials. God is as intimate as the loving word *Father,* yet totally *Other. The unknown, the hidden, the beyond.* No one dare take this name lightly, utter it vainly, use it for selfish ends. It is a name to be loved with all one's heart, soul, mind, and strength, yet never said aloud. The Great Teacher knew and practiced this. We have lost it in our easy familiarity. Hallowed be this name, silent be our lips when we remember this name, dumbfounding be the name of God.

Mystery four: the kingdom: *"Thy reign come."* How does one invite the coming of a reign which contradicts all earthly kingdoms? *"Thy will be done."* How does one surrender to a will which contradicts all human willing? These are the questions of which theology is made, but they are the issues from which all ethics should be constructed and all our daily lives faithfully lived.

Mysteries five and six: breaking bread and broken relationships. The earth-shaking connection of food and body and nourishment for relationships is unique to the prayer of Jesus. Do not miss it—*daily bread AND daily forgiving are* inseparable. The two elements linked together by the only conjunction—the word *and*—cannot be divided. To sit at the table of God, one must sit beside all others. So forgiving is as much like eating as prayer is like breathing. Both are life necessities, necessary to our survival; without them life is impossible. Both are gifts which one somehow does not have to deserve. We eat with gratitude, knowing it is all from God's indefatigable grace; we give and receive forgiveness, knowing that it is all from God's untiring generosity. The proper table manners at God's dining board apply equally to both—sharing food, sharing grace.

Mysteries seven and eight: evil and temptation. Evil is no illusion; it is real; Temptation is no game; it has consequences. Choices matter. Decisions endure. Value-free options exist only in theory or imagination, not in life. All choices emerge from character; all decisions express both who and what the person is, loves, and values. To pray the disciples' prayer is to enter a universe of values that places you in community, in relationship to its Lord, in respect to the ultimate otherness and the immediate presence of God. The prayer situates you in a position of yieldedness and submission to God's will, in dependence for God's care, *AND* in interdependence through the reciprocity of two-way forgiving and being forgiven; in a turning from temptation, and in rejecting all that is evil.

This is only a bare outline, only a sketch of the mystery, a hint of the visible clues to the meaning embedded in the few words of prayer. Beneath these themes lie greater patterns—patterns of grace that reveal Jesus' self-understanding, his understanding of God, his vision of discipleship, his portrayal of life in the community of the Spirit.

For two thousand years, the disciples' prayer has been the object of meditations, reflections, homilies, essays, commentaries. In reality, each disciple of Christ writes her own commentary, lives his own interpretation of its meaning every day. Rarely do we have the opportunity of entering each other's commentary of meditation on this deepest spiritual experience. However, there is a rich tradition of devotional writing which permits such deep encounter, such spiritual participation in another's experience of grace mediated through lived prayer. This is such an experience—such a book—and we are privileged to walk in the shoes of its author as we read.

To participate in the spiritual journey of James Fairfield is to experience a kind of goodness. I know well the impact of his life on those near him. For the last half of the sixties decade, we were co-workers as co-writers for the media division of the Mennonite Board of Missions. We became co-travelers in the Spirit, and I found that living, working, and creating with Jim means participating in a rich spiritual journey. His daily walk with God and with his colleagues was profound yet not pious, reverent yet irrepressible, authentic yet beyond imitation or replication, compassionate yet not compulsive, faithful yet puckishly playful. Jim is an original, and in his being what he truly is, one discovers Jim is being the person God intended him to be, as is always true for genuine disciples.

Jim writes out of life lived through pain disappointment recovery healing discovery discipline freedom simplicity vision practicality dreaming and transformation. He savors thoughts deeply. He listens for the illuminating whispers of the Spirit. He is a person frequently surprised by, occasionally overwhelmed by, often astonished by grace. He is—not surprisingly—the face of God's presence to those whose lives touch his.

To read this book is to risk a touch. Risk it! The touch of grace is safe, but it is life-altering.

—David Augsburger
Fuller Theological Seminary
Claremont, California

Preface

It took us a long time and a lot of complaining to God and whoever else would listen before we began to appreciate what a privilege it is to pray. Then Norma and I discovered the most wonderful of all truths: God has an ear to hear and the desire to help us become complete human beings. That made prayer a profoundly important element in our lives. But it took us so long to find out!

Now we have twelve grandchildren. Could they learn what we've learned a lot sooner? Could we help jump-start the process for them—and for others? The hope became irresistible; the result is *The Grace Connection*.

Growth in understanding has to start somewhere. For Norma and me, it began as teenagers in the United Church of Canada.

Later, the people of faith at the Union Sunday School and the founding group of the Baptist Church at Blair, Ontario, gave us a deep and abiding appreciation for the Bible.

Folks at the Lindale Mennonite Church, Edom, Virginia, opened to us new perspectives on the privileges of fellowship and the way of peace. And the Catholics of many backgrounds at the Church of the Blessed Sacrament in Harrisonburg, Virginia, have shown us the roots of our faith.

So many people stimulated our growth in understanding something of the grace of God that it becomes impossible to name them all. Yet in this project I must thank our children and their spouses, particularly Jim for his encouragement, John for theological insights, Debby for her writing skills, Sam for reaction to my views on reality, and Cathy for her down-to-earth thinking.

Finally, profound thanks to my editor, Dave Garber, for his caring craftsmanship and wisdom.

—*James G. T. Fairfield*
Singers Glen, Virginia

How to Use This Book

- *The Grace Connection* is for the personal enrichment of the private reader as well as for persons who want to study the text together in small groups or Bible classes.

- To enhance your study, biblical references are provided in the Study Guide at the back of the book.

- For the group leader or class teacher, the Study Guide provides questions which you may adapt to stimulate discussion. The references point to biblical sources and background material.

The idea of prayer is not in order to get answers from God. . . . The answers come every time, but not always in the way we expect. . . . You will find there is a reason which is a deep instruction to you, not to anyone else.

—Oswald Chambers

∽

I believe in prayer. I believe that prayer can become the most important fact in the life of modern-day persons who are willing to put this religious discipline to the test. . . . No better testing ground for prayer can be found than in one's own personal life.

—John Sutherland Bonnell

• ONE •

Why Pray?

I sat in my car at a stoplight, shirt glued to my back like a wet leaf. It had been a tough week, temperature stuck at the top of the thermometer. You could fry an egg on the sidewalk except that it was so humid it would poach first. It was midafternoon Friday, and I wanted out of town, but I had another six hours of work to finish.

In a car at the light, the woman at the wheel reached back and whopped a child in the backseat. The light changed and the driver behind her leaned on his horn and yelled something. She looked in the mirror and shouted back, then pulled away ever so slowly, baiting the driver behind. I felt quick sympathy for the child, quicker animosity for both drivers. It was too hot; my irritation levels went off the chart.

There's more evidence of our need for grace on a Friday night in rush-hour traffic than at any other time of the week. Put us all together when we're tired and frazzled, and you have an explosive mixture. Instead of grace, you're apt to unleash fury.

I prayed, "Lord, I don't want to work any more today. Get me out of here, the sooner the better." This was not the best of prayers, but I was feeling sorry for myself. A lot of prayers are the "get me out of here" kind. At least I didn't try to make a bargain: "God, if you do this for me then I'll. . . ."

I remember trying to bargain with God when my best friend was dying. David and I had gone through grade six together, and his mother was our teacher. We went to camp together. He taught me how to swim instead of dog-paddle. Together we dug a clubhouse and chopped poplar saplings for a roof.

David and I spent a lot of noon hours that spring playing around the fishing boats in the harbor. Selkirk, Manitoba, is still a watery place on the Red River only a few miles south of its delta on Lake Winnipeg. Back then, fishing was Selkirk's major industry. The fishing boats came in all sizes, some so big they were hauled out on the dry docks on the north edge of town. Some smaller boats were beached on the riverbank nearer our school.

One Saturday morning David went down by himself to play around the boats. A beached fishing dory had an open pipe leading to the gas tank. David lit a match to look into the pipe; the explosion covered him in flaming gasoline. He lived for five days, mostly in agony.

Why did God let it happen? I'm still not sure, but I think it has to do with our independence. We aren't puppets, and neither is God. Things happen to us we wish we could sidestep. Some die young, some die old, and that's life. For whatever chunk of life we have left, we need help, as much as we can get. If that's too simple, I'm sorry. I've never been very complicated except when I'm trying to hide something from myself or my friends.

∽

Back in 1956 I started to learn about prayer. I'd just turned thirty years old, and had dug myself into a midlife crisis. I don't remember it being called that in the 1950s. A person simply ran up against some of the incongruities of life and felt out of whack for awhile.

As we dive into the new millennium with all its anticipated changes, there's still not much we can do about a midlife crisis. There was little to do for it back then. Some people changed jobs, some hit the honky-tonks, while others plunged into depression and did nothing.

I had no idea then what was happening and why I felt so down. I had a wonderful wife and family, and still do. I had a good job, and enough money to do pretty well what I wanted. Yet life seemed less than it ought to be.

From the safe distance of forty years of living since then, I can figure out why life turned so sour so fast. Three years earlier I had been made top man in a distant subsidiary of the family business, so I felt pretty much my own boss. Then two of my older brothers moved into town and took over, and again I was low man on the totem pole.

That was the first layer of the onion. Peel it off, and I see now that I should never have allowed myself the luxury of feeling like top dog on what was a crowded family totem pole. Four older brothers had spent years fighting it out for the spot, and each had carved a place in the pecking order.

The infighting in my family (all these brothers were old enough to be my father) was probably no more intense than in a lot of families. But since they had lived in their own homes while I was growing up alone, I wasn't used to it. I hadn't been a part of it, and I didn't know how to fight like Kilkenny cats one minute and trade jokes the next.

They used to boast about their ability to fight and stay

friends. But when they fought, it frightened the wits out of me. As a consequence, I grew up not wanting to fight at all. Instead, I was enjoying my individuality, and having three years as my own boss was heady stuff.

So there I was in midcrisis, wondering what was wrong. Nothing really was wrong, I was simply coming face-to-face with reality—a much larger reality than I'd been doing business with before.

Somewhere in midcrisis, I began to realize that a mysterious God had moved from background to foreground. Like God does for everyone at one time or another, this awesome Power—whoever that Power is—had staked out a claim on my life. I started to learn something about God and his uncommon reality, and the process hasn't let up since.

I've come to think of the process as finding the Grace Connection for my life, being awakened to a new way of living that continues to shape who I am into the whole person God wants me to become.

Along the way, one of the things I've learned is this: I am part of God, God is part of me, and you and I are part of each other.[1] That is, if we are willing to let our character be shaped by God's power and yield to God's reign.

Talking about the relationship we have with each other and with God is an uncertain business at best. I've studied theology enough to know that we're dealing with concepts hard to put into words.

A person has to be a lot more gifted than I am to understand much of what has been said and written on the subject. Yet of this much, I am certain—God *IS*. Furthermore, there is a way of communicating with God that lets us understand more about reality: about God's nature, about human nature, about the future and the past.

Prayer is a strange idea when you look at it. It is an unusual activity, unlike anything else we do. Prayer isn't outwardly physical, unless we sigh or put our prayers into words and speak them aloud. It isn't always thinking, although thinking is much a part of praying. Feelings and emotions are involved because we are emotional, feeling beings. Since thought and emotion occur, physical processes are going on inside the brain. Yet prayer is more. Much more!

Personal prayer is the communication tool that faith uses to reach through to the reality of God. We believe that God is available and interested in showing us how to live much more benign lives. Because of who and what God is, by faith we can bring his gracious reality into our own experience.

Most people will admit they could use more help in living than they've found. We are able to train each other in physics and biology, but even our best schools can't instill much in the way of patience and mercy. We can learn the protocols for splicing genes, but we can't spell out how to produce integrity and honesty. We can readily teach the skills of war—even to teenagers—but so far we haven't taught each other much of the skills of forgiveness and peacemaking.

Consider this proposal: The kind of elegant grace we need for living together in this world can't be achieved without opening a channel of communication with God, the Source and Giver of grace.

We can almost make a formula for it: G ~ F $\Rightarrow$ R: Grace shines on Faith to produce Rightness. And prayer is the only communication tool faith has to reach out to God.

Rightness sums up everything we always wanted to understand about life. Faith knows that Rightness is there, and thus reaches out to God, who has so much to give, and to grace us with, that he never runs dry. Grace contains everything we need to live a wholesome life—more-than-enough love, ability to forgive, and power to do the right thing when tempted by the wrong.

I believe if you asked a hundred or a thousand or a million people of faith, you would hear the same thing: *through prayer, the grace connection works.* God's grace is always available, every instant, in every situation, and everywhere. Faith can take up grace like a thirsty sponge. The result is always movement toward righting our life, setting it straight, making sense out of nonsense, giving peace where only turmoil has persisted.

Prayer opens the door to God's knock. On the other side of that door are all the ways and means for doing the impossible, such as loving our enemies. The grace of God provides unlimited resources of skills for getting along with others. Walking on water is nothing! Forgiving in a way that can help both me and my enemy to grow—that's a miracle!

With the help of all that lies beyond that door, miracles such as trustworthiness become possible. In truth, with the help of God, all things are feasible: Getting along with difficult people. Coping with tragedy. Moving the mountain of difficulties we face. All things become possible.[2]

God provides the strength, prayer reaches for it through faith, and things start to happen. Good things! From God come good things, always, and not evil things.

You might say, "But I prayed for my best friend, and he died. How is that good?" We all know of wonderful people who have died, leaving those who loved them in wretched grief. This side of death's darkness, it looks like the worst of evils. I don't know what death is like, and I'm in no hurry to find out. I like it here. Yet according to what happened at Easter, there's something vastly different beyond death.

I'm delighted with the hope. In the meantime, what goes on here on this side has to take priority. I take reasonable precautions for health and safety. Yet finally there is nothing I can do about death any more than I could about being born. It's what happens in between that counts, where I can learn what living is about in all its shapes and shades. Along the way, I might even pick up an insight or two about death.

∽

My friend Bert fixed me up with a blind date. I was in pre-engineering at the University of Manitoba. She was a third-year arts student who should have had more sense. But a friend of hers said she knew me, so she agreed. I still remember what Norma looked like when she opened the door that crisp November night.

I was seventeen, a couple years ahead of schedule in college, and she was nearly twenty-one. When she found out how young I was, Norma didn't want to try a second date. Well, one more. It was 1943, and I was heading for active duty in the Canadian navy as soon as I turned eighteen.

On the third date, this magnificent woman agreed to marry me. I can't believe how young and naive we were. How trusting! How much we needed to learn about ourselves and the rest of reality outside of ourselves. But somehow, God made it right. God began to make the two of us one, and began to open up the rest of our lives.

I believe in miracles because there have been a lot of them in my life. Out of all the lovely young women I could have met in Winnipeg, Norma was the one who swung open the door the first time I saw her. She is a clear and exquisite gift from God. I hope I am a gift to her, and that we both are a gift to others.

We have fought. We have been frustrated with each other. We have hated each other sometimes. Yet always the oneness was growing and overcoming our twoness.

Here is another miracle? While I struggled with my midlife crisis, Norma plowed through her own—for different reasons, but with the same result. We both reached out to God with an eager hunger. We found that God had been there all along, loving us.

Human nature hasn't learned much about itself over the centuries. With all the books written by wise people, you'd think the rest of us might have learned something about our need for God's reality. In many ways, civilization is better than it was five hundred years ago, but not enough to change human nature in any significant way. Each generation still starts over again at the bottom. We do not pass on such smarts genetically. Like us, our children have to discover God all by themselves.

∽

How to pray? I think I knew how to pray long before I ever tried. I think everyone knows how. The cry of the heart. The unspoken yearnings of the spirit. The times when we sit and stare out a window as our minds roam in search of understanding.

Certainly open, voiced prayer is one way, but not necessarily the only or even best way. I'm not sure there is a best way. If prayer is the opening of the mind and heart and spirit to Wisdom and Light, then it can happen almost anywhere, anytime. In traffic. During a meeting. Having a shower.

Prayer puts proposals before God, leaves them there, and looks for answers. Prayer questions why certain things happen, asks what's to be learned from them, and waits for guidance.

Prayer understands the guidance we get, makes sense of answers that come, and taps into spiritual power from God. That's how we know which way to step. That's how we can put one foot ahead of the other. That's walking by faith.

Even as adults, our faith is often weak, hesitant, and mixed with doubts. It is distorted by various half-baked beliefs we pick up along the way that do not match the reality God has set before us. So faith needs practice and exercise, trial-and-error experimentation, and solid disciplined work.

Again, that's where prayer comes in. Prayer always exercises faith. Prayer asks advice of God, tries out different ideas about reality, and even argues with God. Prayer says, "This seems like the right thing for me to do. What do you think, Lord?" Then prayer listens.

The significance and value of the Bible is that it confirms the value of prayer again and again. The Bible has never been simply a rule book. It's mostly a collection of biographies, stories of people who have experienced what it is like to live by faith, or not to live by faith. Stories of rebellion are there, too.

We see how faith works again and again in the Bible, and our soul says, "That's it! That's beautiful! That's the way things ought to be!"

We also see the downside, how faith is abandoned and people turn their backs on God's way, to live for themselves. Their lives can look good, with earthly power and perks in abundance. But on balance, there is less desire for wholesomeness and a greater tendency toward evil in its place. All the bad stuff going on around us doesn't happen by accident. It takes effort on somebody's part.

Most of us find ourselves unsure about good and bad, wholesomeness and unwholesomeness. Few things are ever clear-cut cases of one thing or the other. But that's life, too.

We make choices that sooner or later lead one way or the other. Which choice shall we make?

A person with an experienced pattern of open-ended prayer is much more likely to make the right choice. That person is exposed more readily to the resources for choosing the right option. Experience finds out how to reach for spiritual resources from God.

I insist that all this is true, and that the grace of God is all I say it is. Nevertheless, it is something everyone must discover for oneself and in one's own faith community; it is part of the problem for each generation. But I *can* say that anyone is always welcome to explore God's grace and spiritual power. I've never heard or read of anyone being ignored who tried in good faith to experience the grace connection.

That's about where the disciples were when they asked Jesus to teach them how to pray.[3] They got far more than they anticipated. For one thing, the disciples and others were continually astonished at the depth of Jesus' insights.[4] He was an ordinary person, as were the twelve, without recognized theological or rabbinical training.[5]

We can almost hear the questions: How did Jesus get that way? How could he do what he did? How could he know what he knew? How could he pray as he prayed?

As we study and apply the Lord's Prayer, we also can grow in understanding and in spiritual power through God's grace. Then we will have what we need to live as Jesus lived, with the grace and power to do the right thing.

Jesus appeals to a quite different Father God: a strange God and—as it seemed to many of his contemporaries and especially to those in power— even a dangerous, a really impossible God: . . . who . . . identifies himself with the weak, sick, poor, underprivileged, oppressed, even with the irreligious, immoral, and godless.

—Hans Küng

∽

Grace and peace to you from God our Father and from the Lord Jesus Christ.

—Paul, to the Roman Christians

• TWO •

Our Father

A child doesn't know what a father *is*. I didn't. My dad was just there in my life when I woke up in the mornings, and there at the table when we had dinner at night. Because I was still a boy when his other sons were grown and gone, I became my father's companion whenever I wasn't in school.

When he went golfing, I was responsible to watch where his golf ball landed, too often in the long grass and bushes beyond the fairway. He wasn't an outstanding golfer.

He took me along on some of his business trips to Winnipeg. My father was an aggressive driver. His journeys over the washboard gravel highway—in rural Manitoba during the thirties—became road-rally adventures in the big Durant he loved to drive. Always at day's end, we would stop at a soda fountain for an ice-cream cone, some magazines, and a comic book before we left the city.

One day as I was crawling around under a machine, looking for some nails to use in building a poplar airplane, my father came up to talk to the man fixing the machine. I had a hammer. My father's foot was inches from my nose. He didn't know I was there until I pounded his toes with the hammer.

Although I paid for my poor judgment, he still loved me. Likewise, when I stole a fifty-cent piece from his pocket. And when I wore his vest and got some paint on it.

Unlike a lot of kids, I had a father who loved me and cared for me. I know that now. But I wasn't especially aware of it at the time. I didn't tell myself, "My papa loves me." Kids don't think that way. In fact, I had no idea what he thought about, what was important to him, or that he had plans for the future.

Later, after the Navy, I was back at home and about to become a father. There was no college subject to explain who or what a father was. Maybe there was a book or two about it then, but if so I didn't know where to look for such help. I found nothing to instruct me on the finer points of fatherhood. I had to learn what was involved after our own children were born. That's tough on the kids, especially the oldest.

~

Our Father . . . His followers weren't sure what to think of Jesus. He was like no one they had met before. The man had different ideas, different ways of talking about life and about God. The reality he lived in seemed to be so different from the one they knew. And yet . . .

The things he said made such sense. Here was the old religion of Israel, translated into a new freedom. Old biblical laws were transformed into new responsibilities. To be around Jesus was exhilarating. And frightening. New ways can be disturbing. The old has the comfort of familiarity.

Everything about Jesus indicated an unusual awareness of God. He lived as if God lived in him, as if he and his Father were one. He spoke *as if this were the way it ought to be for everyone.* Furthermore, Jesus approached this relationship almost casually. It was as normal and natural as drawing breath and not at all in religious tradition, as some of his contemporaries expected. In their expectation, serious religion ought to be obvious, with special robes to wear and a pious solemnity.

So it's understandable that Jesus made enemies when he suggested that some of the worst kind of sinners were closer to God than the pious.[1]

It wasn't supposed to work that way. On the top of the social heap were the governing families, political officials, priests, and religious teachers. On the bottom, only a little higher than the slaves, were the tax collectors, hired bureaucrats of the Roman conquerors, and outcasts such as prostitutes, beggars, lepers, and others. These were lumped together in Gospel accounts as "sinners."[2] In between lay the great middle class of craftspeople, farmers, orchardists, herd owners, carpenters, and fishermen.

When Jesus attracted some of the middle class, the religious elite began to watch him closely. Then Jesus broke some of their rules, such as eating meals with publicans and sinners, healing on the Sabbath, and even speaking publicly with women. So the chief priests denounced him as a troublemaker, possessed of the devil.[3]

Thus for Jesus to teach this mixed bag of followers to begin their prayer "Our Father" meant at least that the Father would hear the women and the sinners and the tax collectors. They were not to be excluded. God would listen. It wasn't a matter of how much they knew about the commandments of God or how "good" they had been. There were no restrictions. If the leper or the prostitute wanted to learn how to pray, this was the way to start, "*Our* Father. . . ."

Ordinary people saw the confrontations. They compared Jesus to the religious leaders who opposed him and drew their own conclusions. A growing number attached themselves to

Jesus because they began to want his kind of reality, whatever it was.

About this point, some of Jesus' followers began to think of him as the Christ, the coming Messiah-King, the anticipated revealer of God. Long ago it had been prophesied that in Judah one would be born to represent and interpret the reality of God to his people. Was this the man for whom their ancestors prayed?

The Israelites knew a lot about prayer. Some of the followers of Jesus came from devout families where prayers were said before every meal and on the Sabbath. Every town had a synagogue, and one of the functions of the rabbi was to educate all young boys, beginning at age five or six. When they became adults, some of the more pious ones made prayers in public.

Then why did his friends ask Jesus to teach them to pray? What was it they wanted to learn? Likely more was on their minds than the mechanics of prayer, which they already knew. Jesus responds in a brief, focused statement that has become one of the most talked-about explanations in Western history. Tradition calls it "the Lord's Prayer," and describes it as "What the Lord teaches about prayer." It might better be described as "What the Lord teaches about people and their heavenly Father."

Jesus begins it with his vision of a new humanity awakened to their connection to the Maker of history. This new humanity would *always* be what the old was sometimes, a people with robust and caring faith, a faith like Jesus' own. They would be a people of one mind and purpose, since they were of one Father.

Thus Jesus called people from all walks of life. So it's not surprising that many who gathered around Jesus were from the lower classes. Finally, they mattered. Only a few of the elite were humble enough to see what was happening and let themselves be part of it.

The new humanity would include other races as well. Jesus found great faith in a Canaanite woman who argued him into healing her daughter.[4] The greatest faith he met on his travels—greater than anything he'd seen in all Israel—he found in an officer of the Roman army of occupation.[5] To this day, many Christians adapt this centurion's humble words in their gatherings: "Lord, I am not worthy to receive you; but only say the word and I shall be healed."

Many in Israel shared the faith that the Roman officer expressed, the only kind that counts. Throughout Old Testament times, such faith showed up again and again, including an understanding of God as Father of a universal people of faith. Isaiah spoke of it, and also Daniel.[6] Jonah was an early missionary to the neighboring people of Nineveh.

Yet in the time of Jesus, this concept hadn't caught on widely. Examples of the faith Jesus was looking for were still just that: a few examples. So he took it upon himself to emphasize the availability of "Christlike" faith for anyone—including a Roman centurion. Such faith is in a God who is as close to us as this Father of Jesus, a "Papa."

~

Scotty didn't have a father, at least not one who cared. His mother, Stephanie, became pregnant in grade ten; by the time Scotty was born, his father had another girlfriend. Stephanie lived with her mother, Maud, a nurse's aide, so she had some help in getting ready for Scott when he came along.

Bewildered and frightened, Stephanie dropped out of school. For the first six months of his life, Scotty had a full-time mother, as Maud insisted.

Maud asked for extra hours at the hospital so they could pay most of the bills. Then Stephanie got weekend work as a night clerk at a convenience store. Between the two women, Scotty still had a full-time mother.

The two women look enough like each other to be sisters. Middling tall, Maud can still wear a size six. Stephanie's dark hair and eyes reflect her mother's coloring, although in Maud's hair there are enough gray strands to soften its luster.

Maud wishes her husband were still alive; then things might have been different for Stephanie. How did the pregnancy happen? Stephanie had been a good kid. Maud blames herself: if she hadn't been turned inward so much. If she hadn't been so mad at Alec for dying. If she hadn't felt so alone. Young Scotty could do with a grandfather, but since Alec isn't around, Maud figures she has to try harder, for both Scotty and Stephanie.

Scotty's eleven now, and in spite of what the tabloids say about inner-city kids, he is on his way to becoming a statistic of the nicer kind. His school isn't a good one, but he's a cooperative student. He's a normal kid, and like a lot of his friends, he wishes things would get better in the neighborhood.

All the kids who survive have accumulated street smarts, and Scotty threads his way through the gang politics. He doesn't know what the future holds for him, but he knows it'll be okay. It's largely a matter of knowing he doesn't want to wind up in juvenile court. So he keeps his nose clean and works at his studies.

His mother and grandmother have made his home a place he enjoys, most of the time. It's a place of music and laughter and friendship. Scotty likes his mother and grandmother and thinks they're great. Whatever his future, he wants to be like them. Above all else, he doesn't want to wind up a care-nothing jerk like his father.

"Our Father" doesn't carry as much freight as maybe "Our Mother" might for Scott.

∽

The world has been male-dominated throughout history. Men are bigger and can end any debate with women by force. But it's wrong to conclude that Jesus saw only masculinity in God. All that Scott sees in his mother and grandmother, Jesus saw that, and more, in "Our Father. . . ."

God had been called Father by some of the prophets of Israel, not to give God human characteristics but to characterize the ideal response of his "children." As human sons and daughters were to obey their father, so the children of God were to obey their "Father."

However, Jesus went beyond "Father" and used "Abba" or "Papa."[7] It appears that he was deliberately trying to change the picture. Jesus inferred a relationship of intimacy, of oneness, a relationship hard to contain even in the term "Daddy." Characteristics of the best in human relationships were implied: Mother courage, Father strength, Mother kindness, Father fidelity, Mother patience, Father forgiveness.

This "Daddy" is more than the Father of the people Israel. This Papa is for *all*. And the Father's name and character is Love. Forgiveness. Justice. Peace. Forbearance. These are the qualities Jesus finds in the relationship with his Father.

∽

Finally, there's another angle to this, too. When Jesus tells his friends to start praying "*Our* Father . . . ," he is involving them in the process. For a lot of people, prayer means asking for something: "Please let me win the lottery so I can . . . ," or "Make Marianne do what she ought to do." There's a place for petition as prayer, but Jesus has something more in mind.

Think of "Our . . ." and all that follows as reflexive. In grammar, reflexive means the action of the verb is directed back on the subject: "Mary cut herself." Or more to the point, "Peter worried himself sick." We *know* that Peter can worry himself sick. Medical records tell us it happens to people all too often. Can Peter pray himself well? Maybe! We've also been told that a positive attitude, a reflexive and self-involving determination, is quite helpful in the healing process.

So think of what Jesus is teaching his followers as including the reflexive, a self-involving attitude of ownership in the prayer. "This is our actuality we're dealing with. We are inviting ourselves into the presence of *our* Father."

This prayer makes a difference.

Bell's theorem [dealing with quantum physics] not only suggests that the world is quite different than it seems, it demands it. There is no question about it. Something very exciting is happening. Physicists have "proved," rationally, that our rational ideas about the world in which we live are profoundly deficient.

—Gary Zukav

*How happy are the humble-minded,
For the Kingdom of Heaven is theirs!*

—Jesus, in Matthew (Phillips)

*Would you know my name
If I saw you in heaven?
Would it be the same
If I saw you in heaven?
I must be strong, and carry on
'Cause I know I don't belong
Here in heaven.*

—Eric Clapton, after his young son's death

• THREE •

Who art in heaven

The smoke "towered into the heavens," the newspaper said the next day. It rose as though from a million matches. I saw the smoke when I went out to play after Sunday dinner. My parents were as curious as I was, so we jumped into the old Durant sedan, and Father roared down the road toward the pillar of black soot mounting higher into the summer sky. He thought maybe some hay caught fire in a barn. Or perhaps somebody had set fire to some tires, and it got away from them.

Most of Manitoba is as flat as old soda on a plate, so you can see for miles. We jigged west on the first road north of our place. Then north again toward the mounting plume.

"Must be just outside of Selkirk," Father muttered. My mother wondered about a fire at the Asylum for the Insane, as it was called then. "Might be in the laundry," she offered. "Has to be something big."

We had driven about five miles, and by now the sky ahead of us roiled with angry swirls of the blackest smoke, shot through with orange-yellow flames.

"That's the biggest fire I've ever seen," Father exclaimed, the excitement in his voice making it squeak. I sat between them, on the edge of the seat, little hands against the windscreen. It was the first big fire I'd ever seen, and we weren't even there yet.

After harvest in the fall, wheat farmers used to set fire to the big stacks of straw left behind by threshing machines. At dusk, the sky would blaze with fires across the far horizon. But those were puny compared to this mighty conflagration.

We jogged west and north again. Abruptly Dad yelled, "It's the match factory! Look at that!" I know now that my father's voice held only a combination of awe and concern, but suddenly I was frightened.

We were close now, close enough to see the huge wooden building shuddering like a living thing, flames feasting on wooden ribs rising stories high. A pot of sulfur had exploded into huge gouts of yellow sparks, an enormous Roman candle, punching up and out through what remained of the roof and walls.

"This is close enough." My father pulled the car onto the shoulder of the road and climbed out. I sneaked out beside him and grabbed his hand. He stared at the fire, but I couldn't take my eyes off the huge cloud of black turmoil hanging over us. I loved to watch the clouds in the sky, to watch them change from ships to hippos, from camels to cars. But now the heavens were so terribly angry.

As a child, heaven was up with the clouds and the stars. It was a long time before I understood that God's heaven was more *in here* than *out there*.

∽

People who have no questions never find answers. The people who traveled across the country to talk to Jesus always had questions to ask. Jesus seemed to create questions by the way he talked about life—their life and his. He understood what it was like to live as they did, as a Jew under Roman rule. Day-to-day existence was dominated by a despised foreign culture. The Lord God was supposed to be their only king, not Caesar.

It was believed that the Christ, when he came, would reestablish the territorial kingdom of David. So under these circumstances, the response of Jesus was far from what his fellow Jews expected.

Many of his closest friends hoped he would be the leader to drive the Romans into the sea, but Jesus rejected that military role. To him, what the people expected of God wasn't what the Father had in mind; they did not have a proper understanding of reality. The "kingdom of heaven" wasn't anything like their concept of a "nation under God."

Their reality was one of leaders and followers, power and authority, rank and privilege among the nations. So who were the powerful in this other reality Jesus talked about? "Who," they asked, "would be the greatest in the kingdom of heaven?"

Jesus called a little child and had him stand in the center of the group. He smiled at them all and in Aramaic said, in effect: "The truth is, unless you change your whole concept of living and become like little children, you'll never find yourself in the kingdom of heaven."[1]

This may not sound like an answer to their question. So often Jesus' answers took his listeners in unexpected directions. But if you look at it from his point of view, it makes sense. The kingdom he's talking about isn't even close to the one the questioners had in mind.

Do you want to know about leadership? Then look at this child. The kingdom of heaven—this greater reality Jesus wants them to understand—isn't peopled with self-made dynamic leaders, as in this world. What leaders learn of this world isn't much good in the Father's world. Unless we accept that, Jesus says, we won't get far in understanding what the greater reality is like.

That is why Jesus' idea of leadership has so little to do with our ideas about it. He thought of leadership as being helpful, assisting others in their struggles, giving hope and encouragement, standing beside them in their difficulties. If you want to make something out of life, feed the hungry. If time is on your hands, visit the sick and suffering. If you need a challenge, work for justice.

So are we to think it's a matter of doing certain things right and not doing other things that are wrong? This sounds like what Jesus was getting at, but not quite. Again, "doing good things" gives a picture of what the "kingdom" looks like, but the picture isn't the reality. The reality is more, much more.

Living by "doing right" isn't bad. Go ahead and try it. Hardly anyone will object to a good neighbor. We need all the good neighbors we can get. The religion Jesus grew up to appreciate urged his people to live by doing justice and loving mercy.[2] But too many times this was translated merely into "rules to live by," as if life could be simplified to a few hundred situations. If we learn how to deal with these rightly, we win, according to this mind-set.

Life is never that simple. We can train ourselves to recognize what most people call good, and we can restrict ourselves to a life of predictable situations. But that is not the life Jesus is talking about.

For example, Jesus had been taught, "Godly people don't eat without washing their hands first."[3] That's a good rule. Think of all the germs you avoid by washing first. But for some religious legalists, the rule had taken on the meaning that if you ate without washing, you became an evil person. People tend to do that with rules, making them into "do this and don't do that" religion, to make the rest of us uncomfortable, or put us outside their community.

Nevertheless, laws and rules are necessary. We need them to establish civilization and to protect our neighborhoods from social predators, if nothing else. We need to teach one another what is acceptable behavior, and what is not acceptable. But rules and laws are only a small part of existence. There is so much more.

What is our reality? A world of cities and traffic, finding a good job and protecting it, enjoying our time off, struggling to make ends meet, seeing our children safely through school, staying healthy, and enjoying a party with friends.

Jesus pushes us to consider more, more than family and friends and work and the pursuit of happiness. He declares that there is another dimension to life, and without bringing it into focus, we do not really live as we can live. There is the dimension of "Our Father who art in heaven."

∼

Back when he was in first grade, Scotty asked his grandmother Maud, "What's heaven like? Really?" At school, he muttered, "Damn!" when he jammed a finger, trying to put his lunch down on a cafeteria table. As he rubbed his finger, he nearly added worse language, but an older girl waiting to get by commented that he wouldn't get to heaven if he swore. He didn't know if she meant it or was teasing him, but it irritated him enough that he began to think about what she said.

Scotty wondered what heaven had to do with him in a school cafeteria. Once a teacher declared that it was a heavenly day when it was pouring rain. He snickered with the rest of the class, wondering what she'd had for breakfast.

In the music videos, Scotty sees a guy singing about a girlfriend with a body like heaven. And Heavenly Hash is his mom's favorite ice cream.

However, this girl's comment stopped him cold. What did she have in mind? Heaven as Disney World? Unless Maud or his mom won a lottery, he wasn't going to get there either. And if some witchy girl like her was going to go to heaven, he'd just as soon not bother, thanks.

Maud looked at him and laughed. She remembered her Sunday school days back home, when the teacher used a flannelgraph to show kids in her class about the streets of heaven paved with gold. She didn't want to feed that image to Scotty now. She decided less was more, and pulled him onto the chair beside her.

"I don't know what the girl had in mind," she told him. "I guess a lot of people think heaven is a place they'll go to after they die. Or won't go to, because they're bad.

"I don't think you're bad, Scotty. But watch your language, anyway."

～

Like the rest of us, Scotty is going to find out what lies beyond this life when he dies. But not before. There has been a lot of speculation about what comes after death. Jesus didn't speculate. He talked of a time of judgment, separating the sheep from the goats. So in that respect, the girl who spoke to Scotty was close to the truth.

Some religious people will agree with the girl, and insist that Scotty is on his way to hell with the other goats.[4] Others will say she's making a mountain out of a mole hill. Jesus warned people about judging others. He exposed our tendency to make a fuss about the speck in someone else's eye while we're peering around a log in our own.[5]

When Jesus talks about the "kingdom of heaven," it isn't with the imagery of a place of golden streets and ivory palaces in an afterlife. Almost always, he speaks about something that has to do with this life. The Father who is in heaven isn't the God of the dead but the living.[6] Thus Jesus teaches his people to pray so as to allow the Father to open up this life to "heaven."

This is not a heaven far removed but one close at hand. To most of Jesus' contemporaries—as for me at the match-factory fire—heaven was somewhere out there, up there. God spoke to Moses on a mountaintop.[7] Jacob, one of the ancestors of the faith, had a vision of a ladder coming down to him from heaven.[8]

However, Jesus speaks as if heaven is *here*, all around us, an unseen reality in which we can live and move and have our being.[9] As believers, we are a colony of heaven, part of the holy city that God always has under construction right here on earth.[10]

Up to a half century or so ago, reality for us reached as far as the atom and the visible stars. Visions of a wider, deeper cosmos were most often dismissed as unrealistic. A later empire of Marxist thought insisted that God and his heaven could not exist.

The change to a new understanding of reality did not come from religion but from speculative physics. Einstein and Bohr and later generations of nuclear explorers pushed beyond the atom to the strange realm of quarks and muons. There the rules of empirical science lost their meaning. Time and distance needed different explanations. Some physicists even began to describe the new reality in terms formerly associated with religion: wholeness and rightness.

The reality they explore now is timeless and bounded only by itself. We are used to three-dimensional space and sequential time: length, breadth, and height; yesterday, today, tomorrow.

We're used to three dimensions, and then throw in time for a fourth. Some physicists now talk about ten or more dimensions to reality. Is it such a leap of faith to consider a "heaven" dimension?

Jesus told his people that the heaven dimension was his reality—and it could be ours. It included life beyond death, *but it started here and now* and produced a life of vitality and satisfaction that could never be achieved in a three- or four- or ten-dimensional world alone. In Jesus, God's reign had come.[11]

We live among these limited dimensions, and life here can be vital and satisfying for many. Nevertheless, *vital* and *satisfying* are relative terms. There are no measures that enable us to say, "I have gotten all there is out of life."

For others of us, life can be a monumental drag at best and totally depressing at worst. The possibility that such a life—tough as it might be to survive—can become vitally satisfying is worth investigating. This is especially true when there is a quantum leap of reality to be experienced in what Jesus calls the "kingdom of heaven."

As Jesus put it in one of his illustrations, a person who knows such a treasure is buried in a field will sell everything he owns to buy the field. And start digging right away!

*A name is not . . .
a label stuck
on persons or on things.*

*The name comes from within . . .
and must on no account ring false.
It has to express*

*The essence of the essence
the real reason
for the being, the existence . . . named.*

*Your name
is and only can be
Love.*

—Helder Camara

• FOUR •

Hallowed be thy name

Scotty collects basketball cards. He started when he found a Larry Bird card on a supermarket parking lot. His mother told him she'd watched on television when the Celtics beat Chicago, and Bird had scored about 38 points. Scotty was impressed. He's a Bulls fan, and if Byrd could do that to the Bulls, maybe he'd keep the card.

A week later, on his birthday, his mom, Stephanie, gave him a Michael Jordan card and an autographed Scotty Pippen one. It cost her more than she could afford right then, but when she saw Scotty's delighted reaction, she knew it was worth it. Jordan could do no wrong, even when he quit and turned to baseball for a time.

He likes Pippen almost as much, and with a name like *Scotty*, he couldn't help but become his hero. Stephanie hopes Pippen keeps his nose clean. Her son is at an impressionable age. She worries that he gives too much honor and admiration too easily. Those Nikes and Reeboks are apt to support feet of clay.

To "hallow" something or give it glory can be confusing. Pick up a newspaper, and there's not much reverence given in its pages to a midterm president, whatever his party designation. While some may respect a doctor or admire a favorite movie star, that's not the sort of all-out adulation meant by "hallow."

The closest thing we see now is when teen fans scream and tear off their clothes to throw at a rock musician: "I'm yours" seems to be the message. Adults *may* allow themselves a few moments of that kind of fierce devotion on Super Bowl Sunday. Or as alumni during the March to the Final Four.

Thus, what Jesus lays out here tells us a lot about the depth of experience we can expect when we meet God and his reality in prayer.

Without Jesus' insight into God's reality, there isn't a lot to get excited about. Old friends and new circumstances can brighten life in its duller moments. Most of us find some level of satisfaction in living if things are going right. Eating can be enjoyable, which helps to explain the variety of cookbooks and diet books publishers grind out each year.

Yet day-to-day existence is not often stimulating. Some jobs are downright boring. Marriage, meant to be a haven, often leads to a storm of frustration and discord. Having children can be disappointing and even life-threatening. What starts out as an adventure, winds up in anxiety.

Life's beauty gets painted over with graffiti. Along the road we take little time to smell the roses, and then their perfume is likely to be overwhelmed by the stink of traffic exhaust. So what's to feel good about?

Not much! Until we glimpse the light beyond the darkness. Catch the music of eternity beyond the noise. Taste the tang of a new honesty and integrity. Feel the strong heartbeat of a larger life that can gather up our own in its wholesome embrace.

The experience is brain-stretching, heart-filling, and life-changing.

There's nothing magical about it, nothing particularly "religious." Most of us have come close to it when we're caught by a particularly beautiful sunrise or the perfection of a jonquil or the innocence of an infant's smile. Meeting God gathers up those kinds of experiences and adds its own splendor.

In the fascinating children's books, *The Tales of Narnia*, by C. S. Lewis, all the characters who meet the great lion Aslan—representing the Lord of lords—experience the elation, the sheer delight of someone totally magnificent, totally powerful, totally loving. All their petty concerns melt away in humility, and they are left with adoration.

Yet as wonderfully satisfying as it may be, meeting God like this has never been done mindlessly or in a superficial manner. As Moses approached the bush that burned and yet was not consumed, the Lord God warned him, "Take off your sandals, for the place where you tread is holy ground." Like Moses, we're getting close to something of profound significance here; this is holy territory.

Jesus wanted to teach his friends how to pray effectively, and he knew they should approach the process with care. So too for us. We don't approach God lightly or flippantly, but with respect, and with all our antennae up and sensitized.

Jesus' clear understanding of God didn't come only from his training in the village synagogue school. It came from his devout and adoring attitude to the Father. And that is what Jesus is talking about here. When he talks to God, *his* Father, he "hallows" or reverences his name with all his heart. He not only *likes* the name of God; Jesus worships everything about it. He does so for good reason.

God does not demand, "Get down on your knees and worship my name, or I'll pound your ear." Instead, one who has once been in the presence of God can't help approaching God as treading on hallowed ground. One's understanding has forever been changed.

One of the great experiences of God's presence occurred some 2,700 years ago to Isaiah, prophet of Judah. Isaiah, like all the great prophets, felt deeply that the people were going their own way, ignoring God, and consequently heading for disaster. Isaiah knew of the Lord's love for his people. He also knew that too few of the people returned that love.

In the year that King Uzziah died, Isaiah had a powerful vision. He saw the Lord sitting upon a throne, high and exalted, while heavenly beings surrounded the throne and sang, "Holy, holy, holy is the Lord Almighty; the whole earth is full of his glory."[1]

As others before him, Isaiah believed that anyone who looked on the face of God would die. So he could only cry, "I am ruined! For I am a man of unclean lips, and I live among a people of unclean lips, and my eyes have seen the King, the Lord Almighty."[2]

However, God came close to Isaiah not to kill him but to transform his life with a new responsibility. One of the heavenly beings touched Isaiah's lips with a live coal and told him, "Your guilt is taken away and your sin atoned for," forgiven.[3]

Then the Lord sent Isaiah to challenge the people. He was to tell them, "You hear and hear but never understand. You see and see but never perceive.

"So now your heart is calloused, your ears dull and your eyes closed. Otherwise you might see with your eyes, hear with your ears and understand with your hearts and turn to the Lord and be healed."[4]

This seems to describe the continuing situation between God and humanity. The Father wants his communications to be understood, to be heard and "seen," to be perceived. Yet because any contact with God has to be done through a process that is invisible and untouchable, we ignore the process—and the Father as well. We're busy. We're worried and harried and preoccupied. The skills of faith include prayer, humility, obedience, forgiveness, love, justice-making, and peacemaking. All these are worth learning, but learning them takes more time and attention than we think we have.

So we try to get by on a little here and a little there.[5] A little forgiveness, a little love, a little justice. But it doesn't work that way. We can't get the full benefit of the reality of God and his reign in bits and pieces. In truth, we are starving ourselves on the little bits and pieces.

Jesus understood our dilemma. We want God to be a tame lion, to help us on *our* terms, to fit in with our schedules, and live in our diminished reality. That's the only reality we can see with our eyes and hear with our ears. Jesus tried with his life to bring us understanding. And a few got the message that we don't define God: God's reality defines us.

∽

"Hallowed be *thy name*." In Jewish thought, someone's name held all the characteristics of the life led. The very mention of a bad man's name conjured up images of what he did. So today, the name *Hitler* or *Stalin* paints an instant picture of oppression and terror, injustice and genocide.

If you pick your way through the clan histories and the warfare diaries which make the Old Testament such hard reading, you can find the reason it is still read by millions of people every day. Here and there, showing through like a hidden framework, you can begin to see the outlines of God—his character, his "name."

Throughout the Old Testament, certain marks of integrity

are singled out as evidence of God's character: justice, mercy, compassion for the oppressed and widowed, and forgiveness. These are the qualities of "righteousness" and "holiness."

They also are the marks of the new humanity, "born from above."[6] In other words, through the actions and functions of faith, the "new" human becomes inextricably linked to God's character. His character feeds our character. His name-ness becomes our name-ness.

∼

It was years before I figured out why my best friend, David, wanted to bust my face.

About a month before he died from the burns he received when the fishing dory exploded, David caught me after school and told me I'd have to fight him.

"Why?" I asked him.

"Because. C'mon, put up your fists."

"I don't get it. What's this all about?"

David pushed me, and a bunch of kids came running. I turned and walked away toward Beresford's Grocery, where I'd catch my bus for home. David grabbed my sleeve.

"You got to fight."

"Don't want to. Why should I?"

" 'Cause you're a stinker, and I hate you."

"Why? What'd I do?"

He followed me as I ran toward the store. This had been a baaad week. A couple days earlier, a tough little kid in my class took a swing at me when we were playing dodge ball at noon, and I'd stepped on his foot. We started wrestling around in the dust until our teacher dragged us in and gave us both the strap. My wrists still hurt where the leather had raised bruises.

Now David wanted to beat me up. The crowd of kids

trailed along behind, and when we got to the lane behind the bus depot, he grabbed my books and threw them on the ground.

"Now fight!" he yelled.

"No, I won't! You're crazy! Leave me alone!"

He grabbed my arm and a leg and hoisted, and we went down on the gravel. He rolled over and sat on my stomach. The kids hollered, "Fight! Fight! Fight!" Mr. Beresford came out on the stoop behind his store and started walking toward us.

"Break it up! You kids get along home. Come on, you two, get up from there!" He waved a big arm, and David climbed off. First he hissed, "You're a coward," and then ran down the lane.

I yelled after him, "Sticks and stones can break my bones, but names will never hurt me!" All the kids used that bit of doggerel, but I knew then that it wasn't true. David called me a coward because I wouldn't fight and didn't know why he wanted to. It hurt more than all the sticks and stones and punches would hurt.

I realize now that in his eyes, he had "named" me. In so doing, he cast a long shadow on my character. All I knew then was that it hurt, terribly.

For days and weeks, I felt all warped inside. He wouldn't talk to me at school or even look at me. I wanted to ask him again, "Why?" I began to hate David then, what he had done, and what he had said. Then the news came that he had been burned and wouldn't live. I felt I had killed him.

~

The "name" of God is supposed to be shorthand for his character: knowing, just, merciful, patient, loving. One of the astonishing claims of Jesus is now often overwhelmed by the religious aura we have bathed him in. As a human on earth, Jesus saw himself having access to the character of his Father in heaven. In doing so, he found himself in mortal trouble with the religious and political leaders in Jerusalem. They accused him of blasphemy and sentenced him to death.

However, Jesus wasn't making an unprecedented claim. It can be said that the focus of the Old Testament is on the idea that humans-with-faith are in some inscrutable way linked to God, not only by that faith but by birthright. That is, the actions and functions of faith link the person inextricably to God's character, as if born to his name. This means that human beings can live out the character of God, their Father.

King David is the classic example. For all his many faults—and he had plenty—David demonstrated through faith his access to the qualities of God's name-ness. Another example is in the book of Daniel. There the life-forming work of God in one man's life is held up as an encouragement for all.

God listened to Daniel. And to David. Furthermore, he will listen to the prayers of faith from any of us.

∽

It has long been accepted that God communicated his character to his people through commandments. Over the years, some professional explainers of the commandments created a complex ideology that often got in the way of faith. Religion does that from time to time. Jesus rejected the complexity but treasured the basic truth he knew to be there. When one of the religious leaders asked Jesus which was the most important of the commandments, he replied, " 'Hear, O Israel, the Lord our God, the Lord is one. Love the Lord your God with all your heart and with all your soul and with all your mind and with all your strength.' The second is this: 'Love your neighbor as yourself.' There is no commandment greater than these."[7]

The elegance of the commandments tells a lot about the God who gave them to Moses. This God is worthy of being "hallowed."

∼

I've never felt very religious. Or very good. There are so many times I haven't lived up to the kind of person I'd like to be. Too many times I've hurt someone I cared for. Yet God hears me. How can I be sure?

I am sure because I've learned something about God. He doesn't wait until I become good enough. He hears me in spite of my own continuing shortcomings. God is willing to accept me as I am, and he continues to teach me his reality. The more I come to know of him and his kingdom, the more I have learned to love and revere his forgiving and life-changing ways. These ways are terribly important to me now.

I've also come to realize that all people everywhere are loved of God in that selfsame way. Whether we are "good" or not, whether we are aware of that love or not, we all have the opportunity to experience the grace of God.

This is what Jesus picked up on. The manna that fed the wandering and too-often rebellious tribes in the desert gave evidence of the sustaining presence of God for all of the people. All they had to do was eat.

God's character feeds our character, if we'll let him. His name-ness becomes our name-ness—if we'll eat of that bread.

*Just as each of us has one body
with many members, and these members
do not all have the same function,
so in Christ we who are many form one body,
and each member belongs to all the others.*

—Paul, to the Romans

~

*Because we have to sink our individuality in this
community of the Kingdom, our self-love must be
replaced by total love for all who are our
companions. . . . That was why among the host
of Commandments, Jesus singled out two as
supreme, Love of God and Love of our neighbor.*

—Michael Grant

· FIVE ·

Thy kingdom come

My parents weren't churchgoers. As I look back now, my father had few good words to say about organized religion. He attended church only rarely, perhaps once or twice a year, if that. Yet I do remember him listening often to the radio sermons of Harry Emerson Fosdick, broadcast from New York City.

I don't know what my mother thought about my father's religious antipathies. She deferred to my father in so many things, it was hard to tell what she thought herself.

I believe she was the one who insisted I go to Sunday school at the Little Britain United Church, about a quarter mile from where we lived in the country north of Winnipeg, Manitoba.

Mr. Pettis was Sunday school superintendent, a kindly-while-intimidating Presbyterian. In 1925 the United Church of Canada had pulled together Congregationalists, Methodists, and about two-thirds of Canadian Presbyterians, and blended them into one denomination. Little Britain's tiny Presbyterian Church became one of its rural charges.

Our Sunday school class numbered about a dozen, depending on colds, flu, and the fishing season. Like me, most were from families who weren't regular attenders at the little stone church. As I found, even with the stove glowing red from an early morning coal fire, it couldn't warm up a winter morning in Manitoba. So Mr. Pettis had his work cut out for him.

Starting at Christmas, the twelve-year-olds were supposed to be ready for Easter, when our baptism as infants would be "confirmed" with a personal commitment of faith. Between the weather and the never-ending weekend hockey games only delayed by a blizzard, Mr. Pettis couldn't count on many boys.

However, years later when I struggled to understand what life was all about, I found the New Testament Mr. Pettis gave me that Easter. On a page in front, I had laboriously printed, "For God so loved James Fairfield that he gave his only Son, that whoever believes in him should have eternal life."[1]

I had little understanding then of what that meant. Nor did I later in my thirties. Yet in the early hours of the morning, I would go into our living room, turn on a light, pull this little black book from the shelf, and begin to read. It was one of the most unusual experiences of my life, before or since. In that quiet hour or two when I could no longer sleep, my mind, my soul, my very being found nourishment and peace.

The kingdom of God was dawning in my life. I didn't so much bid it come as I discovered that it had been there all along, except that I could not or would not see it or hear of it. For me to say, "Thy kingdom come," was to open my eyes and ears to its reality all around me.

∼

What *is* this kingdom? One thing it is not is a place as we think of places. It's more a condition of the reality in which we find ourselves, calling for a new attitude, a new way to respond

Thy kingdom come • 59

to what happens to us, a creative approach to the hours in front of us. We begin to see ourselves clearly, and after the initial surprise, start living a bigger, more abundant life.

For two years now, Maud and Stephanie have been a part of a group in their community. It's too small to be called a church as churches go, but for the two women it might well be their introduction to the kingdom of God. Stephanie went to a church one Sunday with another young mother she works with. But she felt uncomfortable, not so much with the other people as with herself. She couldn't figure out what to expect of herself. In the small group, she thinks she'll find out.

Church is supposed to be a visible illustration of the kingdom, a light in the darkness. But too often it can't break loose of its own shadows. Stephanie is doing some serious re-evaluating of her life since she began with the group. She hated God for awhile, and hated men, until she realized she hated herself most. The group has helped her begin to unravel some of her inner knots.

They get together for supper and the evening, Thursdays twice a month. It's potluck. Maud brings a couple of her home-built pizzas, and Stephanie buys something from the convenience store she manages now. Usually she offers ice cream, since most everybody likes Heavenly Hash too.

There are about twenty adults in the group. They catch up on the neighborhood news at supper, find out who's got a new job, or who was laid off and is looking for work. They talk about the kids and school and doctor bills. The children rattle around the edges. Three of the adults—all of them take a turn over the year—look after them and set up the evening's games, listening to the adult conversation when they can.

After supper, they spend the rest of the time together in a loose sort of Bible study. When Maud and Stephanie started, the group had a goal of doing one of the books of the Bible every three months. They were finishing Isaiah then. Since it was long, it took them over four months. Since then they've worked through the Gospel of Mark, Amos, Psalms 23 and 51, 1 and 2 Corinthians. Now they're finishing Genesis, another four-monther.

Stephanie bought herself a new Bible and read it completely through the first month she was in the group. It didn't mean much to her except in places, like Ruth and Acts of the Apostles. Since then, she has read bits of it again, mostly the ones going with their studies together.

Five people in the group know their way around in the Bible more than the others. One couple, Nancy and Paul, are surgical nurses at the hospital and took their training at a Christian college. Zedekiah has rabbinical training and calls himself a messianic Jew. He's a civil rights lawyer and a fierce voice for justice. Ed and Arlene are retired missionaries from India and bring an immense sympathy for cultural differences.

After one gathering, Maud told Stephanie she had to believe in God because he'd been there with them. "Did you ever wonder why we don't have one leader?" she asked, more of herself than of Stephanie. "I guess I'm glad we don't. I've learned so much from Nancy. And Zed. And the others.

"God seems to come at us through everybody."

In *Christianity Today*, April 25, 1994, Thomas C. Oden, professor of theology at Drew University, reports on a conversation he had with Pablo, a young blue-collar worker in Cuba.

"The search for meaning is just as crucial as the search for bread," Pablo told Oden. "While the economy around us is falling apart, Christians are living in a state of special grace.... Ordinary Cubans are becoming aware of the church as a life-saving community of hope."

Some believe the kingdom of God won't happen until the end-times, after the devil and all perpetrators of evil are cast into a lake of fire.

Others say the kingdom happens whenever God acts. So that history is peppered with the kingdom of God. It has come, is here now, and will come until the end of time.

When Jesus tells his friends to pray, "Thy kingdom come," he is expecting God's reign to touch their lives immediately. Think of it as a reflexive statement: you are asking to be involved in whatever God's "kingdom" will be. A person who prays "Thy kingdom come" is saying, "I'm willing to have it happen where I am. Bring it out into the open in my life. Push back the darkness with the light of integrity, rightness, justice, and love in my life."

That's a tall order. It's tough to be a light in darkness. Any person who takes on that job alone is going to stand out like a sore thumb. Most of us want to hide in the crowd and let somebody else take the heat of public inspection.

Look what happens to people in the spotlight, whether presidents or sports stars or other entertainment notables. The higher they climb, the more stories are told about them. It seems that most talk-show hosts make their living off the dark sides of celebrities. And if the princess or the president hasn't shown any dark side lately, somebody will put together a story, the more sordid the better.

Who wants to be a light in that kind of darkness? Keep your head down, your tail covered, and don't make waves. In particular, don't try to break the patterns and shades of darkness we've gotten used to.

The one who prays "Thy kingdom come" takes a big risk. Look at what happened to Jesus. He understood the difference between darkness and light, rightness and evil. He walked in the light, and the darkness could not overwhelm him.[2] Even the dark night of death.

The apostle John wrote, "God is light; in him there is no darkness at all."[3] *Dark, darkness,* and *darkened* are terms used over 150 times in the Bible to describe the absence of good or the realm of moral decay. Foolish hearts are darkened; men seek darkness to hide their evil deeds; they say dark is light and light is dark.[4]

When some people have worked at it long enough, they come to prefer the darkness of evil to the light of truth and justice. Their darkness is a night without light. The rest of us find ourselves under the constant pressure of the darkness around us, constantly being persuaded to go along with evil. We are shaped, influenced, swayed, and tempted by countless impressions. But in Jesus, God's kingdom has come, offering a clear choice.[5]

Jesus said, "Love your enemies. Do good to those who hurt you."[6] Yet we prefer to hold grudges, to look out for number one, to take no prisoners.

∽

As I said, it took me years to figure out why David wanted to beat me up. Maybe it was because I preferred not to know. If I did, I might not like myself.

For a while, it hurt that my best friend had turned on me. Then he died from the terrible burns he suffered, and I felt guilty. So I had another reason to bury the problem—until a couple of years ago.

I was writing about a camp we had gone to, David and I. It started out sideways and ended upside down, one small disaster after another. As I wrote about it, I remembered the fight

David wanted nearly a year later, and that we had ended up enemies.

Why? What had I done to generate his anger toward me? Here I was, over fifty years later, trying to puzzle my way out of the darkness I'd wrapped about my psyche.

Then I remembered the combination of David's anger and the wrestling match I'd had with a kid a few days before. That schoolyard fracas had won us both the strap. The teacher had pulled us into a classroom and made us both stand with our hands turned up while she swung a double-layered leather strap from shoulder height.

She whopped the other kid first—I've forgotten his name—and he jerked with the first blow. But didn't cry. I was already fighting tears, and she hadn't gotten to me yet. On the third smack, his shoulders hunched up and the tears rolled down his face. He was a tough little rooster, but the strap was tougher.

When she got to me, I was jelly. I remember I pulled my hand back on her first swing and the strap caught me on the finger tips. That was not a good idea. The second swing landed where she intended, across the base of the thumb and palm. I tried not to blubber. By the time she finished, my hand and wrist were red and starting to swell.

The teacher was David's mother. She was a widow and a little distant whenever I visited David at home, but she had always been kind. Now she'd been unjust, I thought, and so did the other kid. When she let us go, he and I walked out into the sunshine, commiserating with each other, and wishing the teacher would take a hike, at least.

I wonder now what dark things I said about her in the heat of self-pity? What name and attributes I wished upon her? Knowing the other kids, I'm sure whatever I said got back to

David over the next day or two. No wonder he came hunting; she was his only family. And of course he would not repeat what I'd said to justify taking my head off. That would have seemed a betrayal of her again.

Now that I've figured out what happened, I've asked David and his mother to forgive me. It's a little late for them, but maybe not for me.

"Thy kingdom come!"

*Tension arises when there is a particular people
with a special experience of God in the midst of a
society which either willfully or unwittingly
ignores the will of God. The Bible sees the world
divided into two distinct kingdoms. . . .
Wherever the will of God is realized,
God's kingdom is present.*

—Paul M. Lederach

*The Lord has a controversy with his people. . . .
He has told you, O mortal, what is good;
and what does the Lord require of you
but to do justice, and to love kindness,
and to walk humbly with your God?*

—Micah (NRSV)

· SIX ·

Thy will be done

Not many of us want to do what someone else wants us to do. If possible, we prefer to do things our own way, thank you. So saying "Father, I will do what you want me to do" goes against the grain.

I think men in particular find this distasteful. Our natural arrogance doesn't want to follow another mind. We take instruction, but not easily. To allow ourselves to be instructed in how to be a human being—especially a different and improved model—doesn't fit with who we think we are.

We're told, and rightly so, that we shouldn't try to change anyone into what we think they ought to be. We're told that no one going into marriage should do so hoping to change the other. So we don't expect to have to change ourselves.

Paul, the New Testament's busiest writer, admitted to abundant arrogance himself. Yet he saw that in order to be a whole person, it was necessary for him to be changed and shaped by the Spirit of God. He insisted that to live without letting that happen was not really to live at all. A surprising attitude for a man of such chutzpah.

Over the ages, one of the distinguishing characteristics of Christianity has been that doing the will of God is to do his "name" acts of love, forgiveness, and justice with everyone, even an enemy. At least, that's the idea. A characteristic of the Father is to forgive us when we fail, and to show us through our failures how necessary it is to do love, forgiveness, and justice again and again. Until seventy times seven. We are called to do so consistently through the daily experiences of life.

Nobody can say it's easy. In fact, it's harder to say "Thy will be done" and let God's will happen in our lives than to become the president of the country. We've heard it said, again and again, that a person who wants to do anything can do it. We commonly think that with hard work (and a little luck), anyone can be a success in any chosen field: the stock market, athletics, business, and industry.

However, such achievement so often depends upon winning out over someone else. In most companies, there can be only one foreman of a team, one manager in the office. Only one wins the gold at the Olympics. So what are the rest of us, losers?

The competition goes on between those with jobs and those without, between different ethnic origins, men and women, young and old, educated or not. For somebody to be on top of a totem pole, a lot of others are underneath. And one is on the bottom.

Sometimes we get our signals mixed here. Somehow, "justice" gets to mean everybody should be on top. Or nobody should be on the bottom.

Let's not fight about it. As long as there is birth, growth, adulthood, aging, and death, there is always going to be changing levels of achievement, and a constant change in recognition.

Let's also recognize that there will always be followers who become leaders while still following others. Such daisy chains of authority and submission are not necessarily evil. That is just the way things are and always will be.

Nevertheless, how authority is handled or accepted, and how we lead or follow, can be changed by whether or not our spirit is in touch with and led by the Spirit of God.

∽

I remember driving west on a lonely road in Ontario on the final leg of a business trip. It was early in the morning, just after dawn, and I hoped to be in my office by nine o'clock. But I had over two hundred miles to go.

The car, a new light blue '57 Chevy Nomad, had a muscle motor and could really fly. I let it out. I listened to an Ellington song on the radio, whistling the tune and thumping the steering wheel in time to the music.

The road stretched straight as a pole into the distance. About a mile ahead, I saw something on the road that started an inner dialogue of "conflicting thoughts."[1]

"What is it? Not big. Not moving."

I eased back on the gas.

"It's a box, a cardboard box like grocery stores get full of canned fruit." It sat on my side of the road.

"Don't want to hit it. Might not be empty." I pulled the car into the eastbound lane and swung around it, punching the pedal again.

"You really want to leave that there? For somebody to hit? And get killed!"

"No, but I got to keep going or I'll be late."

"Better late than somebody hurt."

"But it's probably empty! And they can miss it."

"What if another car's coming?"

"Then they'll have to stop and shift it off the road."

"You could have stopped."

"But I didn't, okay?"

"Okay. If that's the way you want it."

When I turned around, I could almost see the box in the distance.

"I bet it's empty."

"So?"

"A truck'll blow it off."

"Won't have to. You're going back!"

It was empty. Not even a rock in it to make my good deed worthwhile. I put it on the side of the road.

"Take it with you. Why leave it for somebody else to pick up?"

"All right! I'll take it with me. Can we leave it alone now?"

I made a bigger deal out of picking up an empty box than Jonah did going to Nineveh to save the people and animals.[2] Of course, a classic Chevy isn't a whale either, but I sulked anyway. Until a strange thing happened—something inside me was smiling.

How do we know when we are "doing" the will of God? How do you find out what it is?

I've always wondered how some persons are so sure they know what the will of God is for their lives. They act as if it has been written in big letters across the front of their minds: "Go to the corner of First and Main, and meet the man in the green hat, who will give you a letter. Do not open the letter until you are home again. Then do as the letter tells you."

Years ago someone passed on to me a five-part process he'd heard about. It sounded good to me then and it still sounds good today. It isn't a surefire thing (nothing is), but it makes sense.

1. First, be sure you *want* to do the will of God. It's not always convenient. So give yourself over to the idea, and pray yourself into an accepting frame of mind. That's what prayer is all about: opening oneself to God so your faith can function.

2. Be sure your spirit is tuned in to the Father's Spirit. Here's where the Bible comes in handy. By reading the Bible, you continually upgrade your understanding of the reality God has created. You see humanity in fresh perspective. You get a more realistic picture of the character of God—and his people.

3. As you begin to understand what you think is the will of God for you at the moment, talk it over with other people of faith. Norma gives me pretty accurate feedback, and I've grown to rely on her insights. Be sure that it will be the loving, forgiving, merciful, and redeeming action. If it isn't, you've missed a turn somewhere.

4. Try it out. Take a step of faith, and do what seems to be the right and appropriate thing. You have an idea of what God would have you do, so do it. He won't bite. Somebody else might, but life's like that.

5. Expect the peace of God to follow. If you've done the right thing, you ought to begin to sense the smile of God, and a sense of being able now to move on.

If we explore the lives of the people of faith in the Bible, we'll see that this sort of day-to-day decision-making fits. And the more often it was practiced, the better they became at living as God wanted them to live.

∽

Although the word "God" does not appear in the Hebrew text of the book of Esther, it has one of the epic accounts of faith in the Bible. Mordecai had raised Esther—her Hebrew name was Hadassah—as his daughter. He was a Jew of the tribe of Benjamin, and a minor official in the court of King Xerxes (Ahasuerus). They were among the Jews dispersed in Xerxes' empire, which stretched from India to Egypt.

In the chronicle, Esther is gathered into the king's harem in a roundup of the loveliest virgins in the empire. At about the same time, Mordecai uncovers a plot on the king's life and the schemers are hanged.

Then occurs the event remembered in Jewish communities everywhere to this day. This was an event demonstrating how one person sought and found the will of God for her and by faith took action to save her people.

An up-and-coming politician named Haman finds favor with King Xerxes. To strengthen Haman's position in court, the king decrees that all his subjects must bow to Haman as to a god. So all the royal officials kneel to honor Haman—except Mordecai, who refuses because of his faith.

Haman is incensed at Mordecai's defiance and determines to exact revenge as well as prove he is the most powerful man in the king's court. Haman persuades the king to issue a decree that, on the thirteenth day of the twelfth month, all Jews throughout the empire are to be slaughtered, young and old, including women and little children. And Mordecai!

By this time, Esther has become the favorite queen of Xerxes. Now she faces a terrible decision. Mordecai asks her to intervene with the king. But unless and until the king calls her to him, she cannot safely come into his presence. If she does approach him without being asked, she risks her own death. So she does nothing.

Mordecai reminds her that as a Jew she faces death anyway. "Who knows but that you have come to royal position for such a time as this?"[3]

So Esther goes to the king, fearing for her life. He receives her and asks what he can do for her. She invites the king and Haman to a banquet. At the banquet, the king again asks what she wants, and promises to give her even up to half his kingdom. She invites the king and Haman to a second banquet, at which she will disclose her need.

All this attention feeds Haman's ego. He gloats at his position and power. But then he sees Mordecai, and his hatred flares again. He orders a huge gallows erected so that when the decree to kill all Jews is carried out, he can hang Mordecai on it and enjoy his revenge.

That night the king can't sleep, so he has the records of happenings in his kingdom brought to him. He finds that Mordecai has never been rewarded for saving him from the plot on his life. In the morning, he calls Haman and asks him what should be done for a man the king wishes to honor?

Haman thinks the king is planning to honor him. So he suggests the king have the man dressed in some of the king's own clothes, set on the king's horse, with a crown on his head, and honor him in a parade through the city.

The king tells Haman he has produced a great idea, and commands him to carry it out—*for Mordecai.* So that day Haman must take the lead in honoring his worst enemy. His wife and friends point out to Haman something he already knows, that he's in deep trouble. He has designed the death of the man the king wishes to honor.

That night at the second banquet, the king asks Esther what she wishes him to do for her. She tells him, "If I have found favor in your sight, please let my life be spared, and the lives of my people. If we were just to be sold as slaves, I would not have spoken."[4]

The king is deeply upset. "Who has presumed to do this?"

The queen points to Haman, "This wicked Haman!"

In his rage, the king rushes from the room, while Haman in terror falls on Esther's couch to plead with her. The king comes back into the room and believes Haman is attacking his queen. He calls for his guards and has Haman hanged on the gallows he prepared for Mordecai.

Because his decree cannot be recalled, Xerxes issues another decree to everyone in his empire that the Jews are given the special privilege of defending themselves against anyone who would seek to destroy them. Esther took a chance on her own life, and the threat against her people is nullified.

The story ends with the good guys wiping out the bad guys.

"Thy will be done. . . ."

My ego is like a fortress.
I have built its walls stone by stone
To hold out the invasion of the love of God.

—Howard Thurman

~

I fled Him, down the nights and down the days;
I fled Him, down the arches of the years;
I fled Him, down the labyrinthine ways
Of my own mind; and in the midst of tears
I hid from Him.

—Francis Thompson

• SEVEN •

On earth as it is in heaven

Most of us live somewhere between heaven and earth, at least in our minds, in our dreams, and in our ideals.
Did you ever make a list of the things you hope to do? I've done it a thousand times if I've done it once. I've made lists on paper, lists in my head.

It doesn't even have to have the formal shape of a list. I see a person doing something I admire, and say to myself, "I can do that." And I add the hope or aspiration or intention or whatever else you want to call it to the ongoing keepsakes in my dream cupboard.

Good intentions are at least better than bad ones. But intentions, good or bad, can lie around in a clutter. Too often the piles of hopes and aspirations in my dream cupboard keep me planning for some distant tomorrow instead of living for today. I spend too much time sorting them out and dreaming "What if . . ." instead of picking one out and working on it.

The people I know who lead happy, productive lives are the ones who don't waste too much time with the future. They seem to know what they want from the future and go after it.

Others I've met lead lives of despair because they've lost both their hopes and dreams and worse, the capability of attaining them. Nothing is as sorrowful as the person who has given up dreaming because of being locked into a pattern of life where dreams shrivel and die.

Jesus speaks about this when he tells his friends to pray heaven down to earth. Let the light of heaven scatter the darkness, so we can see clearly how to sort out the good intentions from the not-so-good ones. Allow the Spirit of heaven to ignite the rightness, justness, and loveliness of the best of the dreams. Move with the dream as it grows, and the will of the Father becomes our own. Then the lesser aspirations and ambitions must fade away.

That's what I keep telling myself. I know it's true. The number of times I've managed to hear the will of the Father over the other loud noises of a busy life have always turned out to be wonderful experiences.

Yet life "on earth" is never simple, never captured and subdued to human understanding. Learn one lesson about life, and you face yet another. Each will be so different, even though the differences are not obvious. The lessons we have already learned often do not seem to apply to the new situations. Except this one lesson: pray the will of the Father be done here, now, in this circumstance. And look for the light of understanding to grow.

~

I am named after the patron of one of my ancestors. My grandfather's grandfather was Robert Burns, the Scottish poet. James Glencairn, the earl of Argyle, befriended Burns, and this friendship has been remembered down the generations.

Burns has been admired for his insight into human nature. He sat behind a fine lady in church one Sunday and saw a louse crawl across her bonnet. As he watched the "wee beastie" travel toward a meal, Burns considered the difference between what we think about ourselves and how others know us. In "Address to a Louse," Burns comes to a conclusion (roughly translated):

> O would some Power the Giver give us
> To see ourselves as others see us!
> It would from many a blunder free us,
>   And foolish notion.
> What airs in gait and dress would leave us,
>   Even in devotion.

Reality is like that for most of us, as far from our perception as heaven is from earth. One of my favorite places as a boy lay under a scraggy wind-scoured oak on the banks of the Red River behind our place. Like many of the riverside homesteads in Manitoba, ours ran from the road back to the river in a long narrow strip. My parents and older brothers had begun a small textile business behind the house before I was born. So I grew up with the sound of machinery in our backyard.

Our house lay only a few feet from the gravel highway from Winnipeg to Selkirk. It had been a roadside inn before my parents occupied it. The traffic featured heavy solid-rubber-tired trucks carrying steel from the big rolling-mill in Selkirk. When they pounded by, dust reached into the sky in a squall behind them, and the house trembled. One summer I chewed tar while watching horse teams and draw-shovels scoop a new roadbed out of the prairie dirt. The gravel way was becoming hardtop.

With the highway in front and the growing textile mill behind, life for a young boy held lots of activity, too much at times. Then the peace of the river, almost a quarter-mile back of the mill, beckoned irresistibly.

My closest friend then was Gosh, a black, curly-haired dog of ambiguous ancestry. He came to stay when I was two years old, and as I grew older, we went everywhere together. The river was a favorite haunt. Gosh liked to swim. I liked to throw a stick for him to fetch. I turned over rocks to catch crawdads for bait. We watched fishing boats struggle upstream against the current.

I would also lie under the old oak tree to see what the clouds looked like. For years, my ideas of heaven were shaped by a riverbank sky. Even now, when life becomes overstressed, I think about that quiet spot and the peaceful moments it bestowed.

~

All our myths and legends locate heaven elsewhere, anywhere but here. We don't think of this earth as heavenly—far from it. Who can look at a polluted stream, a pile of garbage, an abandoned building covered in graffiti, and say, "This is heaven"? Yet Jesus has drawn "heaven" down from the heavens and started its heart beating on earth. Reality is within us. We just don't have the eyes to see it as clearly as the ersatz "reality" we've created for ourselves.

The prophets and teachers of the Old Testament longed for the kingdom of God, a reign of righteousness and peace, when the wolf would lie down with the lamb.[1] Jesus knew his friends looked for a future Eden like that, if not on earth, then attainable after death. They asked "When will these things happen?"[2] Like them, we'd like to think the future has something better than what we're living in now. We want a heaven without a world of trouble and anxiety. Our dreams and aspirations become more real than the life we live.

Life after death is a magnificent hope, made certain by the resurrection of Jesus, the astonishing event that shocked his grieving friends onto a new level of understanding faith. They began to recall what he had told them.

What had he said about the "kingdom of heaven"? That it was near at hand?

The most outrageous claim made by the first Christians was that Jesus was God-come-down-from-heaven-to-become-human. The Gospel accounts in one way or another point to the deadly animosity this claim generated among the religious leaders. This was blasphemy, worthy of death.[3]

Jesus' friends didn't understand this while he was alive. They also did not understand the implications.

∽

When Maud came home from the group meeting, she started talking as soon as she got in the door. Her daughter Stephanie and grandson Scotty had stayed home, recovering from a one-day bug.

"How're you feeling?" she asked, hanging up her coat. Without waiting for an answer, she said, "I'm glad you're still up."

She pulled a straight chair from the table and sat facing her family. "We've almost finished the book of Isaiah. Zed read a part where Isaiah asks God to come down and make himself known. He said that's what really happened with Jesus, and we were all agreeing.

"Then Zed laughed and told us we don't believe it, not the way it really happened."

Stephanie coughed and blew her nose on a tissue. Maud handed her a clean one.

"He got us to read in the Gospel of John where Jesus told his friends that he and the Father were one, doing the same work."[4]

Maud's eyes sparkled with intensity. She stood, walked around her chair, and sat again.

"Then Zed pointed out the part where Jesus insisted that his friends *could do the same as Jesus was doing.* In other words, they could be united with Jesus, who is united with God, and pray in Jesus' name.[5] And that's what our faith can do for us.

"I never thought of it like that before," Maud's voice trailed away and a puzzled look took over.

∾

I know the puzzled look. Maud has had a glimpse into the most surprising thing about Jesus and his place in our lives. This was Jesus' reality:

1. He was human,

2. God was his Father,

3. His spirit came to him from the Father, so that Jesus thought and lived the way his Father wanted him to think and live.

4. *Anyone* who is willing to accept the consequences of thinking and living the same way as Jesus, can do so, because the Father invests his Spirit fully, and makes that person one with himself and Jesus.

5. The life that is then lived will be marked with the characteristics of the Father. Reality takes on the Ideal, and the Ideal becomes Reality. Then righteousness *will* triumph over evil. Justice *will* overcome the forces of bigotry and selfishness. Forgiveness *will* bring peace, and love can flourish.[6]

Sounds great! Why hasn't it happened? Some people despair of "religion" at this point. They condemn any attempt to explain and activate faith.

"If it's as easy as that," you can almost hear them say, "why hasn't the will of God been done on earth as it is in heaven? Why are there still war and famine and children dying, and women being raped, and drugs being peddled on our streets?"

That is precisely why God sent Jesus. Because of the wars and famines and tragedies of our streets and schools and broken homes, God has acted. He has created us to be free, to do such foolish, nasty, life-wasting things if we choose. But he has also created for us the way to live on an entirely different level.

God wills us to be free. He also wills us to do his will. Puzzling? Yes, indeed. If God wills righteousness, why is there so much unrighteousness? The answer lies somewhere near this: so that righteousness may be chosen by free people, freely by faith.

One evening we were having a picnic supper at our daughter's home. Children and grandchildren played a fierce Nerfball tag, hurtling past the adults who sat on the porch and in chairs nearby. As happens often, the women had gathered to avoid the men's talk of politics and religion.

Austin, our oldest grandson, is taking philosophy at college. Tough stuff. We got to talking about free will. After we chewed on it till it got ragged, I offered a thought.

For us, free will is like a stick God balances in his hand. We are designed to be held upright by his grace, but we are free to fall away if we choose. He can restore our balance, our uprightness, if we choose to let him do that. God can keep us upright, if we choose that.

Looking at who we are from another point of view, there are at least three kinds of people: those who decide for evil and like it; those who choose God and open themselves to live his way; and those who vacillate and haven't made a clear choice. Yet.

That is why Jesus directs his friends to pray that God's will would be done "on earth as it is in heaven." "Make up your minds," he urges them. "Make up your minds what you will do with your life."[7]

By every breath of circumstance, we are invited to become partners with the Father in whatever he is doing in building his kingdom. We are becoming "stewards of the stars." But first, we are "stewards of earth," stewards of who we are, where we are.

Our will is a problem for us only when we are not at peace with the will of God. If we choose to do so, we *can* think like Jesus, and live in the will of our Father.

Give us
A pure heart
That we may see Thee,
A humble heart
That we may hear Thee,
A heart of love
That we may serve Thee,
A heart of faith
That we may live Thee,

Thou
Whom I do not know
But Whose I am.

—Dag Hammarskjöld

Come, all you who are thirsty,
    come to the waters;
and you who have no money,
    come, buy and eat!
Come, buy wine and milk
    without money and without cost.
Why spend money on what is not bread,
and your labor on what does not satisfy?

—Isaiah

• EIGHT •

Give us this day our daily bread

In grade school, Alden was an impressive hero. He was smart and knew lots of stuff. Wiry and fast, he was the best soccer player in the neighborhood.

He was kind to the younger kids, including me. So when Alden asked me to help him with his Boy Scout project one summer, I leaped at the chance.

Alden wanted to earn his camp-out badge. Being the kind of boy he was, I figured he'd do everything from scratch. When I met him that afternoon at school, he carried everything he needed in a burlap sack, so I couldn't tell what we were in for.

He picked out a spot near the river overlooking the locks. I liked that because we could sit and watch the fishing boats come through on their way to Lake Winnipeg. Alden set his sack on the ground and told me that the first job was to put up his tent. He rummaged around in the sack and pulled out a bit of old canvas, a couple of straight sticks, and some binder twine.

Alden reached into the sack again and pulled out his

hatchet. He'd made it himself from a piece of tire iron, sharpened with a file, and wired to a green poplar shaft. The boy was ingenious. It hefted like a real hand ax, and had a good edge.

Alden laid the piece of canvas over the spot he had claimed for his tent. At each end he pounded one of the long sticks into the ground. When I offered to help him, he said I was just to watch so he had a witness he did it all by himself.

Then he tied the binder twine to a notch at the top of one stick, ran it to the other, and tied it off. The twine pulled the sticks toward each other. So he braced each end with twine to a couple of short chunks of poplar that he drove into the ground. Finally he hauled the old canvas over the twine and tied each corner to poplar pegs that he pounded in with his hatchet.

The next step was to gather some stones for a fire ring he needed to build. Since I was invited to supper, he figured I could help. We lugged stones until he was satisfied with a circle of big ones, filled in with smaller sizes.

Alden grubbed around in his sack, pulled out a tin pan, and suggested that if I wanted to eat, I'd better get some water from the river. Trusting he knew what he was doing, I happily filled it with the murky water. He had a fire going. I didn't see him rub two sticks together, so he probably used a match. He put the pan of water on three stones in the center of his fire.

Then he stuck his head in the sack again to pull out a paper bag. He held it up, brown hair ruffled, brown eyes flashing.

"Supper," he declared.

I was hungry and full of hope.

"What you got?" I asked.

He dumped the bag's contents on the ground. Green beans. I took the bag from him and looked in. That was it. Green beans!

"Yep. Picked them fresh just before I left. I'll boil them up, and we can eat as much as we want. Bet you're hungry."

I was never hungry for green beans, but if that was all there was . . .

Alden dumped the beans in the water and stirred them around. The pan wasn't big enough, so he poked the beans once in awhile to duck them into the water, which seemed to be slow in getting warm.

The fire needed more wood, and I was delegated to find some. I found a few bits of dead poplar and some hawthorn twigs and poked them under the pan, nearly putting the fire out.

After a long while, steam began to rise from the pan, and Alden declared the beans ready to eat. Whether the water ever boiled is moot. We were past being ready to eat. Alden had a couple of sharpened sticks to poke into the beans to eat with, like one-armed chopsticks.

The beans tasted pretty raw to me, but as I've said, I was not accustomed to eating them. So I could not consider myself an expert on their edibility.

I ate about as much as I could stand, only a handful. Alden ran out of steam about halfway through his portion, about enough to take the edge off his appetite. That's what saved us, not eating any more than we did.

About twenty minutes after the fire had gone out, I began to suspect I had a fire going inside. Cramps! Getting bigger and bolder by the minute.

I began to hate green beans with renewed fervor. I told Alden I had to go home. He decided that would be a good idea for him too. He didn't even take down his tent. I wondered later if he ever did get his badge.

As soon as I got home—about as long a mile as I've ever

walked—my mother fed me some watery mustard in a spoon. It got down there in the midst of the beans and brought them up into the light again. And again. Several more times.

My father thought it must have been some of the dusting powder on the beans. Mother voted for the river water, not boiled enough. I didn't particularly care which one was right.

My parents sat up most of the night, holding my forehead as I retched more beans, even their memory. Along toward morning, I fell asleep, and the worst was over.

I'd rather eat bread any day.

∼

One day as Jesus stood with his friends in the temple, a widow came in and slipped her only two coins into the offering box for the poor. Jesus pointed out to his listeners that she gave far more than the wealthy men who made their offerings out of affluence.[1]

While the rich had plenty left to call their own, she had nothing. The widow had given of her very being; she turned whatever "independence" the money might have given her into dependence upon God alone.

Dependence and *independence*. Powerful words. Each contains a host of meanings for different people.

Most of us allow ourselves to be dependent only when it won't interfere with our independence. I'm a man, and I understand how nice it is to have a wife who cooks the meals, washes my clothes, does the shopping, cleans the house, and feeds my independence. For years I took that for granted. Norma and I grew up in an era when a wife was expected to fulfill that role, to submerge *her* independence as the husband actually depended on her.

We were glad in that I was able to earn enough so we didn't

Give us this day our daily bread • 91

need two incomes. Norma stretched every dollar until it squeaked. She made the girls' dresses. She bought and restored old furniture, even stripping seven layers of paint off a Hoosier cabinet we bought at an auction for $12; it's worth a hundred times as much now. She baked whole grain bread, and ground wheat for breakfast cereal.

We gathered wood together for her cookstove, another auction buy. The stacks of pancakes she built on that stove were some of the finest food I've ever eaten, slathered in her homemade applesauce.

We had sheep, and she and the children looked after them while I worked at my day job. She had a garden, and she canned vegetables and fruit as fast as the children could pick them. Her cold room held about five hundred jars of snap beans, limas, corn, soup stock, spinach, applesauce, peaches, dill pickles, sweet relish, blackberry jam, sauerkraut, apple jelly, pears. She kept a freezer full of breads and pastries, peas, wineberries, and a variety of meats.

However, others, especially some other women, wondered why she didn't have a job.

Our children got little help in going to college; they worked their way through. Maybe it was easier then. I tell myself that, partly because our four children turned out to be such hardworking people. So I can let myself believe that by not helping them much, I strengthened their independence. We only go around once, and I can't turn the clock back to do it over again.

One thing is certain—all of our children are working hard to help their own kids prepare for the future. Each is discovering one's own understanding of dependence and independence. Like balancing a stick on your hand: you can hold it up with your strength, but it may move in any direction it chooses to.

We can choose to be "balanced" by the Father, or we can choose to ignore our dependence and go our own way. In fact, it is far easier to go our own way than to learn to teeter on his hand and move as he moves.

We go to school, learn a trade or profession, and often do it all without any real sense of being led to the right job. The paycheck comes hard and goes easy. Credit cards offer tomorrow on a silver platter. We lease a car, play the lottery, and rent a life. We feel that we're as independent as anyone else. Everybody's in the same boat, aren't they?

Yet once in a while out of the corner of our eyes, we catch a glimpse of a better quality of life. We sniff a passing aroma, like fresh-baked bread, of a greater freedom we don't know how to grasp. We hear the music of the heavens in a baby's laugh and wonder if we'll ever find such free integrity again.

~

I don't know anyone who doesn't wish life were simpler. Our days get overcrowded with all that we want to get done. There doesn't seem to be time enough.

So Jesus' advice to live one day at a time and not worry about tomorrow and its problems, hits the nail on the head. But we have to plan for tomorrow, right? So at least we have to think about what's coming. Then we get to fussing about whether we'll get finished with today's agenda before tomorrow is pounding in on us.

How much busyness is too much? I think it depends on who you are, and what kind of busy-ness you take on.

My problem is that I think I can do everything, so I try. Eventually I become overwhelmed by the amount of work there is to do. So I bury the most important work under a blizzard of less-important, insignificant activity. I circle around

Give us this day our daily bread • 93

doing the unimportant while the one thing I should be doing sits and waits and gets old and changes. If I ever get to it, the timing is off, and the reason it was so important has shifted.

There have been people like me since the beginning of time, crowding their days with chaff. Jesus says, Focus on the one thing most important of all, the reality of God and his timing, his priorities, his agenda. Then if that's our basis for living and working, everything else will fall into its rightful place.[2]

If we keep our focus simple, if we look for just the essential—our daily bread, then we clear the way for clean, crisp, uncluttered action. We will have eaten the one thing we need; anything more that God sends our way is gravy.

A young man came to talk to Jesus. He had a lot of money, lived well, and was a good citizen. Yet he knew there was something more, something eternal about life that he was missing. What more could he do?[3]

Jesus threw him a curve. If the man wanted to get in touch with reality again, he'd have to do something drastic. Jesus told the man to sell all his possessions and give them to the poor. Then he would find himself free enough to depend on God.

At that, the man turned off. This was impossible advice. He had business responsibilities, real estate to look after, a position in the community to uphold.

Then Jesus made his classic comment, "It is easier for a camel to go through the eye of a needle than for a rich man to enter the kingdom of God."

Jesus didn't want his followers to miss what had happened. The disciples wondered that if a man as decent and law-abiding as this one had a problem finding eternal life, how then could it be possible for anyone?

Jesus reassured them. Don't worry, he said, all things are

possible with God. But Jesus had made the point: it's hard not to trust in wealth. It's easy to become possessed with possessing.

We only need enough for today. That's Jesus' message. Don't worry about tomorrow. It isn't here yet, and today has enough problems.[4] Does that mean we shouldn't have a savings account? No IRAs or RRSPs for retirement?

Generation X is rising through the mists of economic changes that are shaking the world. Some say this is the first generation that will not live better than the previous generation. I wonder what the host of people would say whose lives ended during the Civil War or the Great Depression. Did they have it better than their parents? Generation X is being encouraged to feel sorry for itself, to envy what it might never possess.

Yet every generation has its own mountains to climb. Life is tough. The world eats its young, and its old. It consumes any in the in-between years who wander away from the flock.

A lot of kids on the streets have been persuaded to carry a weapon, perhaps influenced by television violence. There is the age-old reality that gentler people tend to ignore: the world eats its strays. So they join a gang, buy a gun, or a dagger, like Romeo and his Shakespearean gang. Behold, there is nothing new under the sun.

What Jesus tells his followers to pray for seems startling: Trust God for your existence, day by day. Don't seek power in this world. Instead, live in the reality of God's kingdom. Our world pushes us to believe in the power that comes from wealth, assets, a stock portfolio, and making the right connections.

Of course there's power in money. How much a person makes has a great deal to do with ease of living, continued good health, a comfortable place to live, and other symbols of achievement. But as Jesus warns repeatedly, the kind of deadly power that money-hunger exercises can cut us off from the simple basics of trust.

Consider the birds of the air, Jesus asked his friends.[5] They don't worry about their next meal. What makes a mockingbird color the midnight air with such magnificent sound? Such a gift cannot be bought. And only a pure trust can give it away to the night so freely.

Consider the wildflowers, Jesus added.[6] Their beauty is not the product of factory politics or one-upmanship.

One day last fall, I drove past a clump of bittersweet growing on a pasture fence. Now that the county doesn't spray the roadsides with herbicides any more, the birds will sow bittersweet along a few more fencelines. I stopped and cut several sprigs to add to our Thanksgiving table. Their unusual color will bless our eyes and lift our spirits all winter.

God clothes the wildflowers. Are we not as worthwhile as they? Jesus insists that God loves us even more than the birds and the wildflowers.

We are at the apex of Creation. Our Father has something far greater in mind for us. To miss that purpose by getting caught up in a turmoil of concern about money and power and prestige is to lose out altogether. We would miss the magnificence of what we were meant for. If we spend our days and nights living for what the Bible calls "the things of the flesh," we're dead to the real life we could be living.[7]

It can be tragic to eat nothing but the goodies and miss the bread of life.

*Happy are those whose transgression is forgiven,
Whose sin is covered. . . .
While I kept silence, my body wasted away. . . .
My strength was dried up
as by the heat of summer.
Then I acknowledged my sin to you. . . .
I said, "I will confess my transgressions
to the Lord,"
And you forgave the guilt of my sin.*

—Psalm 32 (NRSV)

*Mankind is so fallen that no man can be trusted
with unchecked power over his fellows.
Aristotle said that some people were only fit to be
slaves. I do not contradict him.
But I reject slavery
because I see no men fit to be masters.*

—C. S. Lewis

• NINE •

Forgive us our trespasses

Guilt is hard to live with.

The men who worked in the woolen mill behind our house brought their lunches, some in paper bags, others in pails. Leslie Loutit kept his in one of those long black metal boxes with a shaped lid to hold a thermos. I was fascinated by the way it opened up to wrapped sandwiches, wafting smells of an onion or a piece of apple pie, and the thermos warm with hot tea. At noon I would often slip into the shipping room where Les worked and watch the ritual as he would settle himself on a pile of blankets, open his lunch box, and select a sandwich.

A gentle, cheerful man in overalls, Les was one of my favorites. He let me watch him wrap parcels of blankets in heavy paper, crease and fold the ends, then tie it all securely with twine. He had a way of twisting the twine in his palm and with a quick snap breaking it where it crossed itself. At my request, he showed me how to do it, but my little four-year-old hands were no match for the heavy twine.

My mother prepared a big meal at noon for my brothers and father and for any businesspeople from Winnipeg. There was no restaurant anywhere near us in the country, so it fell heavy on my mother's shoulders to feed a dining room full of people.

Midday meals were not my favorite time in the house. My father saw to it that I followed the rule "children should be seen and not heard." So I often ate by myself in the kitchen beside the big cookstove. I much preferred to watch Les open that intriguing lunch box, pull out his tea, and sink his teeth into the first sandwich. Nothing could be more elegant or satisfying.

One day several wool and shoddy dealers from Toronto descended on the mill and I knew I was in for another dull meal by the stove as Mother flew around feeding them. I wandered into Les's shipping room and watched him wrap and tie parcels. Maybe he'd tell me one of his stories. Instead, he asked me to look after the place while he went to bring in a special order from the weaving shed.

As soon as the door closed behind him, I ran to where he kept his lunch box. There it sat, black and shining and closed around a much finer meal than I believed I would get. The temptation was greater than I could bear. I grabbed it up, fled from the room, and ran to the wool storage building.

In the unlit shed where huge bags of wool piled up to the distant rafters, I was alone. I climbed into a corner, wiggled down behind a sack, and settled the lunch box before me.

The moment could not be rushed. I reverently opened the box and sniffed the wonderful aroma that met my nose. There was cinnamon and something else exotic that I could not identify. Without touching anything under the waxed paper, I counted three sandwiches and saw what looked like a chunk of cake as well as a piece of pie.

I picked up the first sandwich and pulled off the wax paper. Two big slices of homemade bread held a thick layer of pork and beans. I took a bite. Delicious! The juice from the beans ran down my chin. I wiped it off, then wiped my hand on the wool sack.

By the time I finished the sandwich except for the crusts, I wasn't too interested in the others. But the pie still looked good. That's where the odor of cinnamon came from, dusted in the sweet apple filling. My mother made a wonderful apple pie, but this slice tasted all the better coming out of Les's lunch box.

By the time I finished the pie, I was content. The tea didn't interest me, so I closed the box and lay back against a sack. Then my contentment began to come apart.

In the distance someone was calling my name. Les? No. One of my brothers. Then another more threatening voice: my father! Coming closer.

My father knew I liked to play in the wool shed. It was a great place to climb and bounce and tumble. The door slid open. "Jimmy? Come on out. I know you're in here!"

"And bring Les's lunch box."

When my father spoke in that tone of voice, there was no choice but to obey. I picked up the lunch box and peeked over the wool sack. He saw the movement and gestured fiercely.

"Come on now." Father's eyes weren't as fierce as his voice. I took courage. "Come down out of there! And don't break his thermos."

I don't remember being punished. Mother and Father exchanged smiles when he marched me into the kitchen.

"I don't expect you want anything to eat?" my mother asked. I shook my head. She offered me some milk and made me sit down by the window, "where I can watch you."

"You mustn't steal other people's lunch boxes," she told me sternly. "Then they won't have anything to eat. It's wrong."

I could see Les eating at the table with the businessmen. He looked at me and frowned. I wondered if he would be quite as kind to me ever again. And I became aware I had made an extra mouth to feed for my mother.

"I'm sorry, Mother. I won't do it again, honest I won't."

"I want you to say you're sorry to Les." Mother looked at me closely. "Do you understand?"

I felt a huge rush of shame. This was much more serious than I thought. Mother took my hand and propelled me to the table where Les sat with all the men. I couldn't look at him. Mother nudged me, twice.

"I'm sorry, Les. I'm sorry I took your lunch." One of the other men snickered. I looked up at Les, and he had his hand over his mouth.

"I won't do it again, I promise." He nodded. My father waved a hand to my mother, who pulled me gently away, but I twisted to look at Les.

He nodded again, and I could see a smile in his eyes. He took his hand down and his smile made me feel all right again. I pulled away from Mother and ran back to hug his knee.

"I really liked the bean sandwich, thank you." Even my father smiled then. It was the first time I really knew what it was like to need forgiveness, and to experience the wonder of being forgiven.

∽

"Forgive us our trespasses." Every day we need the forgiveness and renewing of God, just as we need daily bread. To trespass is to move into someone else's space, and that's what sin is all about. Sin, even the most secret kind, is never private. It is always social, always a trespass against someone else.

I've needed to be forgiven any number of times since stealing Les's lunch. Sometimes I've done it almost unconsciously. But too often I've hurt someone else deliberately, purposefully, and only much later accepted the fact of my ruthlessness.

The parking lot at our county library has an entrance for cars from both ends. I was in a hurry, peeled into the lot, and saw another car coming from the other direction. He was heading for a space at my end and was already signaling his turn. But he wasn't moving fast enough, and I beat him to it.

Only after I got out of my truck did I recognize the man in the other car. When you don't know somebody, it's easier to cut him off. But I knew Ray, and he knew me. He often sat in my Bible study class, and that made it even worse.

How do you apologize for being a snake? Not easily. But Ray was gracious. I still remember his smile. It was sincerely warm and forgiving. I don't remember all he said, but he let me off the hook: "Looks to me like you're in a real hurry, Jim."

I told the story at the next Bible study. I was in a hurry, and willing to push a stranger aside to meet my timetable.

The sin wasn't so much in what I did, although I stole Ray's parking spot. The greater sin was in my attitude, rating my time as more important than his.

If Jesus had been on the scene, he would have peeled some bark off my ego. He might have said something like "Woe to you, teacher! You clean the outside of the cup, but inside you are full of pushiness and aggression. Who do you think you are, anyway?"

Thank God for forgiveness. I'm still learning how to deal with my aggressive nature, channeling it properly so I can get things done. But if I let my shoving get in the way of others, I need to back off and seek forgiveness. The world has more aggression than it can handle now. The push for power becomes an addiction, using others to feed the voracious hunger that is never satisfied.

~

David is Israel's most impressive king. He had become a heroic figure, creating a nation out of distant and differing tribes by muscle and diplomacy. While absorbing other cultures and peoples, David rejected their household and local gods to uphold the God of gods, the One Lord.

Yet David drifted into power-addiction and through it to murder most foul.[1]

David had sent his army to destroy the Ammonites while he remained in Jerusalem. Unable to sleep, David walked on his rooftop in the cool of the night. Looking down, he saw a beautiful woman bathing in her garden and wanted to possess her.

He exercised his power. Find out who she is, he ordered. He was told she was the wife of Uriah, one of David's soldiers on the battlefront.

David had the woman, Bathsheba, brought to his bed. He was king. She was a woman, and furthermore only a soldier's wife.

Back at her home, Bathsheba discovered she was pregnant and sent the news to the king.

Now David engaged in another power play. He had Uriah brought to him. After hearing the news from the front lines, David sent Uriah home for the night so he would sleep with Bathsheba. But instead, Uriah slept in the servants' hall.

David sent him home again the second night. And again, Uriah slept on his mat in the servants' quarters. "Why should

I sleep with my wife in comfort while my fellow soldiers are risking their lives?" he asked the king.

So David, now totally out of control, issued orders that during the fighting, Uriah be put in a place where he would be killed. As a result, several other fighting men were also killed.

David arranged this just so he could take Uriah's widow as his wife.

As Lord Acton said over a century ago, "Power tends to corrupt, and absolute power corrupts absolutely." David heard from God through the prophet Nathan: "You let sin take over, and now you must accept the results of the choices you made."

David repented in sorrow but paid the price. Sadly, so did the child, who died. Others usually suffer when we go wrong. There were other consequences: Solomon, the son Bathsheba later bore to David, became his successor. Although fabulously successful by worldly standards, Solomon laid heavy taxes on the people and married foreign wives, who brought along the worship of many gods.[2] He thus set up the kingdom for division and its long decline.

∼

The first wish of an erring child climbing onto Father's lap is for forgiveness so that a loving relationship can be renewed. David's spiritual legacy is not in how he ruled or failed to rule but in his search for forgiveness.

David created Psalm 51 after the prophet Nathan challenged his adulterous and murderous actions. It is an exceptionally beautiful prayer and one that has brought hope for forgiveness to millions of transgressors over the centuries.

> Have mercy on me, O God,
> > according to your steadfast love;
> according to your abundant mercy
> > blot out my transgressions.
> Wash me thoroughly from my iniquity,
> > and cleanse me from my sin.
> For I know my transgressions,
> > and my sin is ever before me.
> Against you, you alone, have I sinned,
> > and done what is evil in your sight. . . .
> You desire truth in the inward being;
> > therefore teach me wisdom in my secret heart.
> Purge me with hyssop, and I shall be clean;
> > wash me, and I shall be whiter than snow. . . .
> Create in me a clean heart, O God,
> > and put a new and right spirit within me. (NRSV)

There is a delicate balance between ego strength and humility. We need to be strong in order to exercise the gift God gave us, but never at the expense of another person's growth. In the eyes of God, nothing we do has any meaning apart from what we do with and for others.

As God's chosen ones, holy and beloved,
clothe yourselves with compassion,
kindness, humility, meekness, and patience.
Bear with one another and,
if anyone has a complaint against another,
forgive each other;
just as the Lord has forgiven you,
so you also must forgive.

—Paul, to the Colossians (NRSV)

Our Father, . . . help me to be an instrument
of [yours by] returning good for evil,
returning soft answers for sharp criticisms,
being polite when I receive rudeness. . . .
So may I, in gentleness and love,
check the hasty answer,
choke back the unkind retort,
and thus short-circuit some of the bitterness
and unkindness that has overflowed Thy world.

—Peter Marshall

• TEN •

As we forgive those who trespass against us

Stephanie has a male friend who wants to live with her, no commitments. A lot of couples are avoiding marriage, he says. It's too confining if it turns out you aren't compatible. Vows aren't what keep a couple together. Who needs somebody else's permission to live together, anyway?

The man's arguments are persuasive, and Stephanie can't quite find the holes in his logic. But she feels sure there's a reason for the commitment of marriage. She can think of a few good reasons herself: We tell the world we have made a choice till death do us part. It takes a commitment to permanency in order to survive the times when you vehemently disagree. There is truth to the idea that two hearts, two lives, and two spirits become one in a way we haven't really understood yet.

Maud thinks her daughter will do the right thing, so she hasn't said much. She wants to warn Stephanie, but she's afraid she might spoil the process of discovery going on. The man is jealous of Stephanie's son, and Scotty knows it. But Stephanie has ignored the situation, until now.

Stephanie has been lonely. She doesn't understand the young girls today who have a child and don't want to marry the father. It's a cultural twist she doesn't grasp at all. She loved Scotty's father with a teenager's romantic passion, and when he left her, she couldn't—wouldn't—forgive him. When she had to bear Scotty alone, the hurt ripped a wound that ran deep in her spirit. She couldn't trust a man near her for years.

Now she is beginning to understand. When she had sex with her high school sweetheart, she was bonding in the way she wanted to live for the rest of her life. After he left, she invested a lot of her love in Scotty, and it seemed enough. She wonders now if that's why many teenage girls have a baby: they don't hope to get from their man the lifetime commitment they'll get from their child.

Now Stephanie realizes marriage is much more complex than sex. She sees the kind of relationship some of the couples have in their Bible study group, and her old romantic ideals have been reawakened. She sees that a man can be strongly committed to a lifelong relationship, and she has begun to wonder what the future holds for her.

She hasn't talked about this with Maud. She has hardly admitted to herself that she has been thinking about marriage. And she has made up her mind to dump the man who doesn't believe in commitment.

The first thing she has done with her new understanding is to forgive herself for her past. She is also forgiving Scotty's father, wherever he is and whoever he has become. She'd tell him if she knew where he was or if he ever showed up. But at least, he's forgiven. Her heart is free now, and that's a magnificent thing in itself.

Stephanie is free of the wound she clung to for all of her adult life. She is free to look at her world in a different light, and she is seeing so many things about herself that she wants to explore. So she's not going to get into another relationship that has little to offer beyond the first night or two.

Forgiving has allowed Stephanie to let go of the past, a past she has dragged along like shackles. Now today has taken on new value, and tomorrow is possible again.

∽

Because I had done some research and written a manuscript on stress, I was asked to give a talk to a group of pastors. I didn't think too many would be interested. Yet when the door closed on the last pastor, the classroom was full, with standing room only.

Obviously, stress was a major factor in their overly busy lives. All of them were men, and they complained of not having enough time for their wives and families. They were on call all the time. People demanded too much of them. Each pastor felt he was expected to be at every meeting, no matter how trivial, and give leadership to youth, care for the sick, prepare excellent sermons every week, handle the finances, marry, and bury—and have an impeccable spiritual life in spite of the pressure.

These overworked pastors wanted a remedy, an antidote for their stressed-out lives. These were well-educated people who had heard about relaxation techniques. They knew of the benefits of exercise and the value of meditation training. They hoped I had found a combination to recommend, perhaps some new therapies to try.

However, would therapies help as much as they wanted? Didn't they need to learn to say no? Perhaps they were doing too much and needed to back off. Sometimes less is more. Wanting to do God's work has a twist to it. Sometimes we believe we have to do God's job, not necessarily just what he would have *us* do. We may think we have to guarantee results and thereby please the church board.

On occasion, even Jesus walked away from crowds who needed him. He knew the value of moving at God's speed. It was important not only for his mental and spiritual state but for his physical health as well.

For these pastors to add a therapy to their schedules might help, but it would not solve the problem. Only a change toward a simpler lifestyle would work in the long term, finding a benign groove of balanced activity. Their busyness was a trespass against themselves. The fallout from taking too much on themselves amounted to a trespass against others and against their own persons.

These men felt oppressed and enslaved although they would never admit it. To admit such a slavery might mean they had allowed their egos to pull them into a no-win situation. They were sent to love and serve a people, but they had let that people become the source of their feelings of enslavement. They felt powerless to make any changes. To them, the congregation had become monster.

As it emerged, the answer looked obvious, but not easy to accept. When we have our days all mapped out by someone else, it's hard to live with freedom and openness to life as it arises. People struggling under that kind of pressure don't have the privilege of doing anything else, unless they can negotiate some changes.

Each pastor would need to acknowledge that he had shared in creating the situation. To find a less-stressful lifestyle, a benign groove where the peace of God could catch up with him, he'd have to make a change in his self-perceptions. Then he could enlist the congregation in doing much more of its own maintenance. He'd need to become selective, doing only the work a pastor should, and involve the congregation in figuring out what that was so he could arrange a healthier schedule.

In any event, it meant a new approach. For each pastor, it meant confronting the congregation with its trespass on his time, then forgiving, and moving on. But as Jesus points out, this is a two-way street. In doing so, the congregation earns the right to confront the pastor with his sins and his need of forgiveness, too.

∽

To forgive as we are being forgiven is tough. To start with, we don't want to think we need absolution: "Who, me? What did I do?" Then we explain to the other person, "You really don't understand the complex nature of the situation, and why I had to act the way I did." We look back on what we have done and rearrange what we see to put the other person in the picture in retrospect. We justify ourselves: "I did what I had to do."

So we don't look for forgiveness, at least not often, and not when we really need it. When we have seriously hurt someone else, if we admit it and seek to be forgiven, that would mean that we commit ourselves to changing the situation. No one really means it if he or she isn't willing to work at healing the hurt or repairing the damage they have caused.

Some people build a shell around themselves: "I am right. Nobody else understands the situation from where I am." The shell effectively prevents them from seeing the other person's point of view.

When a person builds a shell, he excludes others. It becomes a controlling attitude, a hardness of heart that can be spiritually deadly. In the demanding world we live in, such a person loses the ability to hear the voice of God.

∽

Marietta Jaeger knows how hard it is to forgive. She and her family were camping in Montana when Susie, her seven-year-old, was kidnapped. Hours turned into days, with little to help the FBI and local police in their search.

The distraught mother suffered in anguish. She describes her initial hatred for the kidnapper: "I could kill him. I meant it with every fiber of my being.

"I'm sure I could have done it with my bare hands and a smile on my face. I felt it was a matter of justice."

Weeks stretched into months. There were no new clues, except for a few calls from the kidnapper. As the story is told in *Catholic Update,* he offered to exchange Susie for a ransom, but never proposed how the exchange would be made.

Who could think of forgiveness at such a time? During those dreadful months, Marietta struggled to maintain her sanity.

"My Christian upbringing," she explains, "and my knowledge of good psychological health had taught me that forgiveness was not an option, but a mandate."

It was perhaps the hardest thing she has ever had to do. "I argued and argued with God."

Finally she gave God "permission to change my heart." She began to pray for the kidnapper.

Fifteen months after the kidnapping, the man was arrested. He faced the death penalty, but Marietta asked the prosecutors to settle instead for life imprisonment with psychiatric care.

Only then did the young man tell what had happened to

Susie. He confessed that within a week of the kidnapping, he had raped her, then strangled and dismembered her body.

Why did Marietta forgive him? Why did she not urge the death penalty for the killer of her seven-year-old daughter?

She believes in the grace of God. It doesn't mean she advocates parole and release to the streets. "I know there are people who should be separated in a humanely secured manner from the community for the protection of all." But she did not want her daughter's death to bring about another death.

As she explains, the death penalty would not have eased her burden. "No number of retaliatory deaths would compensate for the loss of my daughter's life, nor would they restore her to my arms."

She believes forgiveness alone removes the torment and bitterness. Vindictiveness and retaliation in kind only gives the offender another victim, she insists.

A short time after his confession, the kidnapper committed suicide.

∼

A lot of us would not be able to forgive as Marietta Jaeger has done. But there is no question that this is the kind of forgiveness Jesus had in mind. He even forgave his own executioners.[1]

If you were to sift through the Bible for an understanding of the nature of God, you would have to admit that *forgiving love is* his most important characteristic. Jesus defined it and gave us a clear challenge:

> You have heard that it was said, "You shall love your neighbor and hate your enemy." But I say to you, Love your enemies and pray for those who persecute you, so that you may be children of your Father in heaven. . . . For if

you love those who love you, what reward do you have? Do not even the tax collectors do the same? And if you greet only your brothers and sisters, what more are you doing than others? Do not even the Gentiles do the same?[2]

This may be the toughest part of living in the way of our Father. When we've been hurt, when people we love have suffered at the hands of another, forgivingness and loving the "enemy" are next to impossible. In our anguish and anger, we hardly know how to pray. Yet even here grace steps in as the Spirit of God himself intercedes for us with "groans that words cannot express."[3] In our weakness we are made strong, for then the grace of God can be our power.[4]

When we are forgiving, we offer and live out peace to the enemy. Thus "enemies" can only be enemies in their own attitudes and actions, not in our outlook. When asked by Jesus to "love" our enemy, we are not asked necessarily to like the person. We're only asked to be willing to forgive. Feelings of "liking" have little to do with forgiveness. They may come later, if at all, during the process of reconciliation. Then the enemy responds and also begins to be concerned with the distorted relationship.

So, Jesus says, children of the heavenly Father are forgiving. Yet offered forgiveness can be received only when those who have offended sincerely repent and set out to change, with God's help. They have to get their life out of reverse before they can go forward.

Forgiveness is the tool of faith to bring about union with our Father and each other. As humans, we are interconnected. Without forgiveness, there is no avenue to reconciliation and community.

That's what "redemption" or "salvation" is all about, forgiving and being forgiven. Forgiven for all that we are—and all that we are not.

However much we forgive what has been done to us, God forgives all similar trespasses in us—and so much more. God forgives entirely and completely. He forgives *all* our transgressions.[5]

This is how to pray always. So that we are renewed and set on our way, God's way, no matter what has transpired in life up till now. We are set free of the past and made alive for tomorrow, renewed in God's likeness, as his children, made strong with his strength to do the right, to live in love and justice.

*I thank thee, Lord, for forgiving me, but I prefer
staying in the darkness: forgive me that too.*

*No, that cannot be. The one thing that cannot be
forgiven is the sin of choosing to be evil,
of refusing deliverance.
It is impossible to forgive that.*

—George MacDonald

*Why do we consider that "good" is better than
"evil"? Surely this recognition of good, so deeply
rooted and so universal,
is another . . . pointer to Reality.
Both beauty and goodness . . . exert an effect
upon men which cannot be explained
in terms of the world that we know.*

—J. B. Phillips

• ELEVEN •

Lead us not into temptation, but deliver us from evil

Scotty came home white-faced and trembling. There had been another drive-by shooting near his school that afternoon. He'd seen two kids lying in a pool of their own blood.

"They went to our school," he told his grandmother. Maud, about to leave for her shift at the hospital, pulled Scotty to her and held him close.

"Somebody said the guys were probably dealing drugs and got into a fight over territory." Scotty took a deep breath. "But they were good kids. I think they got hit just because they were walking on the street when the shooter went by."

Maud's voice had an edge to it. "And the shooter'll never get caught. The bad ones go free while the good ones die young."

This wasn't the first shooting in the neighborhood, and it wouldn't be the last. She hated what it meant for Scotty and for all the children at the school. She prayed for them every day. She felt that was the most important thing she could do on her own. Maybe God would show her what else to do.

Evil so often triumphs. A drunken driver swerves onto a crowded sidewalk, plowing a swath of mangled bodies. A drug dealer offers a free hit of crack to kids; it's his basic training program. A man sexually molests his baby daughter—and son. A mother tells police her two children were abducted by a carjacker, then confesses she has drowned her babies in a lake.

There but for the grace of God are we. Evil calls out to evil. Our hearts may respond through malice or jealousy or lust. We may take up evil to gain advantage or revenge. If we do so, we are in the wide stream of destruction that has torn lives apart down the centuries.[1]

People don't start out purposefully evil. It takes practice, here a little, there a little.[2] Even doing good for the wrong reasons is a step toward a hardened heart. Once the heart is stony hard, not much will get through to soften it.

Yet there is the grace of God—but God doesn't push. If we aren't willing to be turned around, he isn't going to do it for us. In that case, we'll continue to build a hard heart and live a hardening life apart from all that is gracious and gentle and ennobling.

Is this God's fault? Does God lead us into temptation and evil? Is God responsible for the things that tempt us?

Not at all. There is a peculiar construction in the original language that throws the meaning of "lead us not into temptation" back onto the previous phrases. In a way, it's reflexive: "Forgive me as I forgive, so I won't be led into temptation and do evil." If we do not forgive, we set up a problem for the future, a rock in the current of time. It creates an eddy, disturbing the flow of our days with disharmony.

Lead us not into temptation, but deliver us from evil • *119*

We are what we do. If we don't forgive, we are shaped by that attitude. We become unforgiving, we become *hardened,* and we are led into temptation. What we become affects others around us, spouses, children, friends, and business associates. They sense our bitterness, see our wariness, and taste our animosity. Their responses are shaped accordingly.

This part of the Lord's Prayer could be called the focal point. It is certainly its culmination. Temptation is serious business, but temptation-becoming-evil is far stickier. Its attempts at beauty are more distorted, seductive, and demanding. It's addictive and won't let go. Without God's grace, we are helpless before its strength.

∽

If you've ever tried to give up smoking, you'll know what an addiction this temptation-becoming-evil can be.

I started to smoke cigarettes when I was fourteen. It was the thing to do. All of my buddies started about then. We would light up on the way home from school after football practice. Learning to inhale was a heady rite of passage.

My older brothers all smoked. It was believed to be relaxing and good for the digestion, as the cigarette commercials told us again and again. Lucky Strike sponsored the Hit Parade and thus connected with the fun times that young people had with music.

Back then in the '40s, smoking was even patriotic. Free cigarettes were shipped to soldiers and sailors overseas. There were no smoke-free areas in restaurants. If you had a problem with cigarette smoke, you suffered in silence or left the room.

When I started, a pack of cigarettes lasted me a week. Yet by the time our last child was born twenty years later, I was inhaling two or three packs a day. I was really hooked.

I made a few halfhearted attempts to cut back, but none of them worked. One day I faced a four-hour evening flight from Toronto to Winnipeg for a number of business meetings. I stuck a ten-pack carton of cigarettes in my briefcase just before I left for the airport, and opened the first pack on the way.

In Winnipeg, one of my brothers met me at the airport and took me to my motel. The two of us talked—and smoked—until about three in the morning. I was in the first meeting at 8:00 a.m. As the day progressed, I needed to replenish my pocket supply of cigarettes from the shrinking carton in my briefcase. At 5:00 p.m., another meeting started. I reached for another pack and received a severe jolt: I pulled out the last pack.

I had worked through that carton in a little over twenty-four hours. No one else in the meetings smoked my brand. The others all favored mild Canadian cigarettes that I thought were too moist. I preferred a drier smoke and chose a particularly dry American brand.

Later that night on the flight back to Toronto, I determined to quit, cold turkey. It turned out to be the hardest thing I've ever done in my life!

Addiction? Yes. Temptation-become-evil? You bet.

As usual, I craved a smoke first thing in the morning, as soon as my feet hit the floor. Everywhere I went, people lit up and blew wondrous gales of smoke in my face. I didn't need to light up myself; I could just breathe enough smoke to stay hooked.

I chewed pencils, and gum. I twitched my fingers at ashtrays. I followed smokers like a bird dog. But I didn't light a cigarette. Tough as this was, I knew if I ever started again, I'd never stop.

Did it get any easier as the weeks went by? Not much.

Even six months later, I was still fighting. But there began to be days when I never thought about a cigarette. Gradually the days lengthened into weeks. Then months.

Looking back, I know now that if God had not helped me, times without number, I wouldn't have lasted a week. Smoking killed one of my brothers with lung cancer. It was a mean and nasty death. So I figure anyone who manages to quit, or who never starts smoking, achieves a terrific victory.

～

Anyone who has been "delivered from evil" knows this. It's as slippery as an eel. Evil twists itself into the shape of something we desire. It can taste so good that we want more and more—until it has control over our lives.[3]

Over the centuries, people have tried hard to put chains on evil with laws, community sanctions, police action, and social pressure. Groups have attempted to define behavior: "This is the way we do things. If you choose to do otherwise, we will turn our backs on you."

Such external control has always fallen short. The group may succeed in coercing behavior so that everyone may look and talk and act alike. But under the surface, evil remains. And evil rubs its hands with glee.

Laws and rules are essential to human community. Without them, we would be ruled by chaos. But laws and rules cannot produce in us what we don't have a heart for.

～

When the small tribe of Israel's children settled in Egypt, they prospered at first. They saw it as the blessing of the God who had revealed himself to their ancestor Abraham.

However, somewhere along the line, the Egyptians began

to see them as a curse, as foreigners taking food from their mouths. Gradually the Israelites were maneuvered into poverty, then abject slavery. The biblical story of Exodus tells how God delivered them from bondage and began the process of forging them into his "demonstration people." They would become a model program, showing the world how humans were to live in a loving relationship with the only true God.

Nevertheless, it wasn't an easy apprenticeship. People who have been used to living without the extra demand of listening to a *holy* inner voice don't make the best of pupils. Anyone can dream up an inner voice, but rarely a holy one.

To help them out, God spoke through Moses and delivered some basic commandments for the people, so they could check what they were "hearing." This was the way to make sure that what came out of their hearts and minds would be the living law of God. It would entail personal righteousness and interpersonal justice.

As soon as the Israelites escaped Egypt and found themselves totally dependent on God for food and water, many began to long for their life in the "good old days" of slavery.[4] Some grumbled that God had led them into the desert to tempt them. The people of that generation were scarred by their former lives. They were hardened in their unbelief. All God could do with them was to minimize their influence on the next generation.

Because of the grumblers, all the people spent forty years meandering in the desert of Sinai. They had to move at God's pace, follow where he led them, and live on the bread he provided day by day. In spite of the hard, rebellious hearts of many, some did learn to live in that unusual state we have come to call faith.

All through the turbulent history of Israel, many refused to

Lead us not into temptation, but deliver us from evil • *123*

acknowledge God or lost themselves in the twisted superstitions of the people around them. Yet a number grew in the wisdom and understanding of the God of love, forgiveness, and justice.

Today we stand at this end of a long line of people of faith who lived in awareness of God and submission to this one God. These people are of every nation and culture. And we're still learning what God is all about.

We're still discovering the strength and power of his grace in a world troubled deeply by temptation. While our temptations always have an effect on others, they come at us on a personal level. We eat and drink too much. We think too much about sex. We feel superior to others. And we don't know how to change.

However, the grace of God is greater, and it's always available. All we need do is reach for it and cling to it. Evil can surge all around us, *but by the grace of God, it cannot touch the soul.*[5] Even if the body is destroyed—and it happens that way sometimes—the spirit of a believer remains safe with God.[6] Death seems to be the greatest evil. We resent it bitterly and fight to stay alive. But it is only the end of our time here. We move on to the triumph of a newer and greater opportunity.

On the other hand, if we let ourselves be swept up by evil, if our very souls are caught up in evil and given over to it, then we are already destroyed. There is no hope, no life. The hell we have built here on earth is already eating us with its fires of jealousy and rancor and viciousness and greed.

One of the unique features of Christianity is the death of Jesus. It is the central reality of our faith, the scandal of a just man put to death unjustly. Be sure of this, that Jews of faith did not kill Jesus. It was a few leaders more concerned for their own power and position in this world than for the kingdom of God. It became the temporal conquest of self-centered pragmatism over righteousness, of evil over humility and integrity.

The execution of Jesus was a clear demonstration of the presence of evil in the world. Yet his death was also verification of something far greater: God delivers from evil.

I don't understand what happened in those hours and days after Jesus died. How does someone return from the dead? Let's not waste time trying to establish any kind of rational explanation. That can't be done. Nevertheless, the impossible happens, and somehow *Jesus lives*. The demoralized, frightened group of people who had followed Jesus are lifted out of their fear and sorrow and loss of hope. Jesus comes to them in the flesh, convincing them of the triumph of faith over evil forever.

Ever since, in innumerable ways, the lives of multitudes, all people of faith, have proved the power of the resurrected life. They show that God will not allow us to be swept away by the corruptions that surround us. If we walk in his strength and commit ourselves to his life, we are free.

Even in death, we are free. So what of the hells that life throws in front of us? What of pain and sorrow, anguish and despair? Through them all, even through death, life and release beckons.

That is why the writer of the final book of the New Testament tells of a million million voices around the throne of God, singing in exultant triumph.[7] It is their truth. They have proven what is real: GOD IS. And his name is Love, Forgiveness, Justice.

God has chosen to offer the resurrected life of love, forgiveness, and justice to as many as call on his name.

*The Spirit which Jesus promised would lead
his followers "into all truth" is very actively
at work wherever he is allowed.
Some of his work is painful in the extreme. . . .
Anyone who opens his personality
to the living Spirit
takes a risk of being considerably shaken.*

—J. B. Phillips

*Now to him who is able to keep you from falling,
and to make you stand without blemish in the
presence of his glory with rejoicing, to the only
God our Savior, through Jesus Christ our Lord,
be glory, majesty, power, and authority,
before all time and now and forever. Amen.*

—Jude (NRSV)

• TWELVE •

For thine is the kingdom, the power, and the glory, forever and ever. Amen.

We don't hear much about the good things going on in our world. Instead, the news media fill us with drive-by shootings, the latest celebrity divorce, and the megabuck salary of another professional ballplayer.

Yet all around us are the grace-filled stories of ordinary people. I met Paul at the University of Florida Medical Center in Gainesville. Four of us were in the one room. Paul was tall, lean, well-muscled, and possessed of a quiet faith in God. That faith gave him a serene courage that calmed my apprehensions.

All four of us faced major surgery within days, and we pushed for details from each other. Wayne and I were there because of cancer, George for heart repair, Paul for the restoration of his bowel after a terrible accident.

He had been a lineman. When his safety equipment failed, he fell from the top of a pole to land on the spike end of a tree. The top had snapped off in the same storm that brought down the power line.

Paul was impaled through the anus, up through his intestines. The spike of the tree stopped just short of his heart. He was conscious all the time the crew cut the tree and lowered him to the ground.

That had been four years and nineteen operations ago. Over a hundred splinters had been found in his abdominal cavity. Sections of his torn bowel were patched or removed. Infections were fought and pain endured. Now the hope of returning to some semblance of a normal life lay on the other side of the next operation—if it worked.

Wayne and I were scheduled for cancer surgery on our upper arms. My surgery was more painful, perhaps, and his more disabling. Also a man of faith, Wayne was a bank executive from Knoxville. The lump on his humerus gave him considerable pain, but our surgeon had dealt with this sort of invasion many times before. He would remove the bone entirely, from shoulder to elbow. For the rest of his life, Wayne would have a floppy arm, but there would be a useful hand at the end of it.

Wayne spoke softly and sparingly but with calm confidence in the outcome of the operation. His wife, Betty, kept up a constant cheerful chatter that he seemed to enjoy. We were roommates also after surgery, mine first. The only time Norma saw any wavering of his equanimity, and of Betty's, was when two slight nurses brought me back to the room and tried to shift me from the gurney to the bed. Barely conscious, I wasn't coherent, and the pain was monumental. My groans and yells must have shaken them severely.

∼

I have a feeling that most miracles are private, at least while they're happening. As Norma and I sat in the waiting

For thine is the kingdom, the power, and the glory forever • *129*

room at the orthopedic clinic at the University of Virginia Hospital, we talked about it. In the crowd of patients around us, we wondered how many other private miracles were happening.

Back in 1970, a tumor fattened itself on my left shoulder. Too obvious to ignore, our family doctor recommended that it be removed. After the operation, the general surgeon pronounced it benign. Since he was sure he had removed all of it, we were confident that we likely wouldn't see it again.

Four years later it was back, and a second general surgeon cut it out, again pronouncing it benign.

Two years later it was growing again. This time the same surgeon inadvertently cut into the tumor, because all he removed was—in his words—"a bunch of funny looking fat."

After four months, the familiar half-grapefruit bulge was back. Our son Jim, a physician in Lansdale, Pennsylvania, expressed concern about this "nonreturnable" tumor that kept returning. He advised us to go to an orthopedic surgeon. Too much was happening too close to sensitive areas like the neck and a lung.

The miracle started to happen. We went to see Irvin Hess, an orthopedic surgeon in Harrisonburg, Virginia. He hustled me into Rockingham Memorial Hospital and operation number four, six months after number three. The surgeon warned us afterward that the tumor cells seemed intimately associated with some of the nerves controlling the shoulder. One nerve in particular bothered him since it penetrated the humerus, the upper arm bone. He hadn't gone after it because he didn't want to do more damage to the shoulder than necessary.

Previous lab reports from the University of Virginia Hospital declared the tumor benign. But this time Dr. Hess also sent tissue samples to the pathologists at the national tumor center in Bethesda, Maryland.

Sometimes miracles get worse before they get better.

Norma got a phone call from Dr. Hess. The biopsy reports were in. She arranged an appointment for us to see him at his office.

When he walked into the examining room, his face told the story. The tumor center identified the growth as a liposarcoma and advised that "more tissue be taken."

Now came the dicey part. What next? Dr. Hess said he'd like us to get a second opinion from the University of Virginia Hospital.

So there we were, in the crowded waiting room at the orthopedic clinic of University Hospital in Charlottesville. Waiting. After four operations in seven years, with intervals much shorter each time, our waiting had taken on a strong sense of apprehension.

We were living under a brooding cloud. The tumor haunted me when I woke up at three in the morning. It was there when I quit work for the day. It was a lethal "little shadow that goes in and out with me" (R. L. Stevenson). We were waiting and wondering and praying without ceasing.

People who are enjoying an instant miracle don't sit around apprehensively. They leap to their feet and shout, "I'm healed!" or "I can see!" and get it over with. Our case wasn't working like that. I suspect most miracles take all the waiting we have patience for, until we recognize what God is doing for us.

We had to wait some more. An appointment was set up with Dr. William F. Enneking, a specialist in tumors of the extremities, coming up from Florida the following week.

I had a book manuscript to finish, so Norma dug in to investigate who this Enneking was. She got our son Jim on the phone again. Yes, he had a friend in residency with him who had studied at the University of Florida. The friend was "wildly enthusiastic" about this "best man in the field" and said we were fortunate indeed to connect with him.

Norma also found Dr. Enneking listed in *American Men and Women of Science* at our local library. So we were expecting a medical celebrity, one who would breeze in, pronounce his opinion in lofty medicalese, and leave us in even greater confusion.

However, a real miracle always involves authentic people. Dr. Enneking walked into the examining room, introduced himself, and sat in a chair next to us. His tweed jacket was a little baggy, his shoes somewhat scuffed, and a smear of plaster on his trousers showed he had been busy with a cast.

As a cancer specialist, Dr. Enneking has seen thousands of cancer cells under a microscope. Before our meeting, he had looked at the tissue samples from all my previous operations. He identified malignant cells in even the earliest tumor. Now the situation was much more threatening. We waited for his opinion.

"You don't wait for this kind to come back. You go after it immediately and get rid of it." If the migration of malignant cells was not checked, the consequences would be life-threatening.

The tissue in question did follow a nerve into the humerus. It would be necessary to remove the top one or two inches of the bone, depending on further tests. Also, all the shoulder muscles and nerves would have to go, and the arm would be reattached to the muscles of my chest and back.

He would arrange for me to be admitted in ten days at the hospital in Gainesville, Florida, if we could make it there by then. He warned that I would feel like I'd been hit by a truck and would be out of commission for months. Afterward, I would have limited use of my arm, but it would be better than no arm at all.

That may have been one of the lowest points. Although there were many other lows of intense pain, that day is etched in memory as one of the longest in our lifetime together. We agreed to his schedule. Then we stumbled out into the sunshine, stunned and cold from shock. We were trying to digest the implications, waiting for the confusion of anxiety and dread to wane, and coming down from the adrenaline high.

Again that evening, we talked to son Jim. He didn't seem surprised. He affirmed our decision as the only one available.

That was twenty years ago. The pain has faded. With Norma's encouragement, I have learned to use my arm all over again so well that most people don't notice it's two inches shorter than the other, or that one shoulder isn't as broad as the other. I have much more use of my arm than I dared expect.

The experience has done more to demonstrate to me the kingdom and the power and the glory of God than anything else in my life. For a start, I respected Dr. Enneking's conviction that he was only a participant and that God was the healer. The men from Lindale Mennonite Church came to mow the grass, saw wood, wash windows, and fix a sagging gate. We survived the financial drain with the help of Mennonite Mutual Aid.

For us, the experience holds all the evidence of our Father at work in precise provision of just what was needed at the precise time of need, and to meet that need through people.

What more could a miracle be?

For thine is the kingdom, the power, and the glory forever • *133*

As we move into the new millennium, we carry over the realities of the old. Our world may be a hell to live in at times, but it is the only one we've got. In it the greatest of opportunities has been offered to us: we can live in the joy and triumph of the grace of God.

The story of the human race is the story of God reaching out to humanity and humankind seeking after God. The Bible is a record of the relationship of God to men and women and children, their stories of faith and lack of faith. It shows us the struggles of ordinary people to believe and follow, but also their destructive tendencies to selfishness and injustice. The Bible is a chronicle of humanity in all its triumphs and failures. Some discover the wondrous grace of God, and others choose to run their lives without that grace.

As I said before, there are few teachers or trainers or counselors who can give us the kind of elegant wisdom we need for living in this world together. If there were enough of those around, would some neighborhoods be such wastelands? Would our world be so full of selfishness? We are able to train each other in the high technologies but not in patience and mercy. We can splice genes but we cannot manufacture integrity and honesty. We are experts in passing on the skills of war but not the powers of forgiveness and peace.

We all have a choice. All the world of ideas and religious persuasion lies in front of us. Is it a competition among truths? Or is it an opportunity to discover our Father, the Father of all truth? It is our privilege to discover God's voice, his leading, and his compassion.

This part of the Lord's Prayer is the response of the person who knows, beyond the shadow of a doubt, that God is pure delight. He is compassion, mercy, equity, and so much more. God is life itself, and death is but the doorway to a new and more mature experience.

We have so much to learn, about ourselves, about cultural differences, and about getting along together. As we move into the new millennium, we are discovering how small our world has grown. How much we need each other in order to survive! We are of different origins and ideas, yet even in our differences, we are alike.

We are like leaves on a tree. We do not choose which tree we are born to, so some are oak leaves, others poplar, and still others locust.

Oak leaves are leathery and tough, deeply colored, hanging on even when dried brown, lasting through winter storms, and falling only when replaced with the new leaves of spring. Poplar leaves, fragile and pale, shifting ceaselessly in every breeze, are short-lived and yet graceful in every motion of life given. A locust leaflet, never single, is always part of a larger cluster of leaves, finding life only in the group.

We are all leaves, knowing intimately the movements of the wind, stirring and leaping, able always to respond, and yet tied to our origins. We live, knowing only the wind coursing through our part of the tree, reaching toward the sun in that part of the tree, soaking in the rain on that part of the tree, waving from that part of the woods.

We become so familiar with the wind and the sun and the rain in our part of the tree, as *my* kind of leaf. So we expect all others to know surely that this is how every other leaf exists and responds, exactly as we do, as *I* do. Yet each leaf's experience is totally different; no two alike. Even those in multiples, leaflets in a leaf cluster, are not quite the same—even though they might insist they are—and can never be the same.

Yet the wind, the sun, and the rain are one to all leaves: one movement, one warmth, one blessing, experienced differently by each leaf, but one nevertheless.

We are different from each other. Thus it may be as hard for us to forgive the differences between us as to forgive an actual wrong against us. Yet the freeing grace of God is available, if we want it. And that's the rub. Some people prefer their prejudices and don't want to change. New freedom isn't as familiar as an old slavery.

That is why prayer is so important. It is the first step in turning things in a new direction, toward a more benign way of life. It is the first step in discovering a bigger God and a more wholesome future. It is the first step to a newer and stronger faith each time we pray, and when we pray the Lord's Prayer (known from church liturgies and in various versions of Matthew 6:9-13 and Luke 11:2-4):

> Our Father, who art in heaven,
>   Hallowed be thy name.
> Thy kingdom come. Thy will be done
>   On earth as it is in heaven.
> Give us this day our daily bread,
>   And forgive us our trespasses
>   As we forgive those who trespass against us.
> And lead us not into temptation, but deliver us from evil.
> For thine is the kingdom, and the power, and the glory,
>   Forever and ever. Amen.

Study Guide and Notes

Personal Bible study is food for the soul. We can be enriched by a thematic biblical study with a group of persons committed to help each other grow in the disciplines of faith. Here are a few questions to stimulate thought and discussion as you read through each chapter. Biblical references keyed to the note numbers in the text provide verification and opportunity for additional exploration.

Study group leader: Reality as kingdom of God will create the appropriate background for study of *The Grace Connection*. Encourage your group to consider the elements of time and distance from any experience. Bad things happen—yet everything about Jesus' life and death demonstrates how God can transform those experiences. *Your goal:* Help your group see that prayer is the means by which we participate in this transformation. Use the questions and biblical references for a sense of direction in your study.

1. Why Pray? Jesus would endorse the idea that unusual circumstances often produce the desire to pray. What experiences in your life have stimulated prayer? If you accept that God always answers prayer, what was the answer to your prayer? What has it meant in your life? What connection does prayer have with other spiritual disciplines?

References: (1) Acts 17:26-28; 1 Corinthians 12:12-13; John 17:20-23; 2 Peter 1:3-4. (2) Mark 10:27; Jeremiah 32:26-27, Genesis 17:15—18:14. (3) Luke 11:1. (4) Mark 1:22; 6:2; 7:37; 11:18. (5) John 7:15; Acts 4:13.

2. Our Father. Jesus tackled the difficulties of parent-like allusions to God in language and terms of his time. How many different periods in history have influenced our understanding of maternal love? Of justice? In what way have paternal values been shown? What is the significance for you of the reflexive action of prayer, changing myself?

References: (1) Luke 18:9-14. (2) Matthew 9:10-11. (3) Mark 3:22; John 8:48. (4) Mark 7:24-30. (5) Matthew 8:5-13. (6) Isaiah 42:6; 49:6; Daniel 4:34-35; 7:27. (7) Mark 14:36.

3. Who art in heaven. Jesus gave new dimensions to old understandings. What new expressions would help your friends and neighbors understand God at work now? What terms would you use to explain "heaven"? Where does God "reside" today? Jesus says the kingdom is among us or in us. How does that locate "heaven" for you?

References: (1) Matthew 18:1-5. (2) Micah 6:8. (3) Matthew 15:2. (4) Matthew 25:31-46. (5) Matthew 7:1-5. (6) Mark 12:26-27. (7) Exodus 19:3. (8) Genesis 28:12-13. (9) Acts 17:28; Luke 17:20-21. (10) Revelation 3:12; 21:2; Galatians 4:26. (11) Luke 4:14-21.

4. Hallowed be thy name. When parents name their children, they often refer to a book to see what meaning tradition has given to a name. What does your family name say about your origins? How important is a "good" name? How does a proper understanding of the reality of God inspire confidence in his "name"?

References: (1) Isaiah 6:1-3. (2) Isaiah 6:5. (3) Isaiah 6:7. (4) Isaiah 6:9-10, adapted. (5) Isaiah 28:10, 13. (6) John 3:3, NRSV. (7) Mark 12:28-31.

5. Thy kingdom come. What differences can be identified between the realm of God and the world we live in? If we don't want anything but the world we've got, why would we choose

God's reign? If we make a choice for the kingdom of God to come in our lives, how might our role in the world around us be altered?

References: (1) John 3:16, adapted. (2) John 1:5. (3) 1 John 1:5. (4) Romans 1:21; John 3:19; Isaiah 5:20. (5) Luke 11:14-20. (6) Matthew 5:44, paraphrased.

6. Thy will be done. Many of us find decisions hard to make, for a number of reasons. How can we become confident that we know God's will? What evidences do we have? How have you discovered the will of God in your own life?

References: (1) Romans 2:15. (2) Jonah 4:3-11. (3) Esther 4:14. (4) Esther 7:3-4, paraphased.

7. On earth as it is in heaven. In what ways can dreams and wishes get in the way of living our lives in the reality of God? Can dreams and wishes be helpful? If God's will is that we be like Jesus, what might that mean for our world? What hinders us?

References: (1) Isaiah 11:6. (2) Mark 13:4; Acts 1:6. (3) John 10:33. (4) John 10:30, 38. (5) John 14:10-14. (6) 1 John 4:12-16. (7) Matthew 16:24-26.

8. Give us this day our daily bread. In a world that demands achievement, how can we live as Jesus suggests, like the birds and the flowers? With family members to support? What is meant by trusting first in God's righteousness? If you were given an extra hour in each day, how would you use it?

References: (1) Luke 21:1-4. (2) Matthew 6:33. (3) Matthew 19:16-26. (4) Matthew 6:34. (5) Matthew 6:26. (6) Matthew 6:28-29. (7) Romans 8:5-14.

9. Forgive us our trespasses. Is it possible for anyone to go through life and not need to be forgiven? Is sin an act or an attitude? Or both? How important to you is the help available from the members of your congregation? Other Christians? The Bible?

References: (1) 2 Samuel 11—12. (1) 1 Kings 11.

10. As we forgive those who trespass against us. What do you expect forgiveness to feel like? If feelings of revenge and retribution are present, can there be forgiveness? How can others help us when the anguish and anger are ours alone?

References: (1) Luke 23:34. (2) Matthew 5:43-47, NRSV. (3) Romans 8:18-27. (4) 2 Corinthians 12:8-10. (5) Psalm 103:1-5.

11. Lead us not into temptation, but deliver us from evil. Why does it seem easier to identify "sin" when someone else is doing it? Why do we find it hard to see it in our own lives? What are some modern temptations the Bible doesn't talk about? What suggestions do you have for hearing and listening to the Inner Voice that is Holy?

References: (1) Matthew 7:13-14. (2) Isaiah 28:10, 13. (3) John 8:34; Romans 6:16-20. (4) Exodus 16:3; 17:3. (5) John 10:28-29; Ephesians 6:16. (6) Romans 8:38-39. (7) Revelation 5:11-14.

12. For thine is the kingdom, the power, and the glory, forever and ever. Amen. Finding God's favor is worthwhile for many reasons. What are the most vital reasons for you? What part of your life may be the most influenced by the presence of "our Father"? What is to you the most convincing aspect of the life of Jesus?

Bibliography

1. Why Pray?
Chambers, Oswald. *My Utmost for His Highest.* Uhrichsville, Ohio: Barbour and Company, 1963.

Bonnell, John Sutherland. *The Practice and Power of Prayer.* Philadelphia: Westminster, 1954. From the intro. Longtime minister of Fifth Avenue Presbyterian Church, New York.

2. Our Father
Küng, Hans. *Does God Exist?* Trans. Edward Quinn. New York: Vintage Books, Random House, 1981.

3. Who art in heaven
Zukav, Gary. *The Dancing Wu Li Master: An Overview of the New Physics.* New York: Bantam Books, 1980.

Clapton, Eric. *Unplugged.* Burbank: Reprise Records, 1992.

4. Hallowed be thy name
Camara, Helder. In *The HarperCollins Book of Prayers.* Compiled by Robert Van de Weyer. New York: HarperCollins, 1993. Camara is a Roman Catholic priest, the archbishop of Olinda and Recife, in the least-developed region of Brazil.

5. Thy kingdom come
Grant, Michael. *Jesus: A Historian's Review of the Gospels.* New York: Charles Scribner's Sons, 1977.

6. Thy will be done
Lederach, Paul M. *A Third Way: Conversations About Anabaptist-Mennonite Faith.* Scottdale, Pa.: Herald Press, 1980.

7. On earth as it is in heaven

Thurman, Howard. *Conversations with God: Two Centuries of Prayer by African Americans*. Ed. James Melvin Washington. New York: HarperCollins, 1994.

Thompson, Francis. "The Hound of Heaven." In *Immortal Poems of the English Language*. New York: Simon & Schuster Pocket Books, 1952.

8. Give us this day our daily bread

Hammarskjöld, Dag. *Markings*. Trans. W. H. Auden and Leif Sjoberg. London: Faber & Faber, 1964.

9. Forgive us our trespasses

Lewis, C. S. *Present Concerns*. Ed. Walter Hooper. New York: Harcourt Brace Jovanovich, 1986.

10. As we forgive . . .

Marshall, Peter. *The Prayers of Peter Marshall*. Ed. Catherine Marshall. New York: McGraw Hill Book Co., 1954.

11. Lead us not into temptation . . .

MacDonald, George. *An Anthology*. Ed. C. S. Lewis. New York: Macmillan, 1947.

Phillips, J. B. *Your God Is Too Small*. London: Wyvern Books, 1956.

12. For thine is the kingdom

Phillips, J. B. *The Ring of Truth*. New York: The Macmillan Co., 1967. Phillips translated *The New Testament in Modern English* and also wrote the best-selling book *Your God Is Too Small*.

Christian Living 34/3 (Mar. 1987) published some material incorporated in this chapter.

McNally, Thomas, and Wm. G. Storey, compilers. *Lord, Hear Our Prayer*. Notre Dame: Ave Maria Press, 1978: the Lord's Prayer as in Rite 2, *The Book of Common Prayer: According to the Use of the Episcopal Church*, Sept. 1979.

The Author

As a communicator, James G. T. Fairfield tries to reach between the seen and the unseen, between life and faith, and explain the spiritual chemistry involved.

He began his career in communications as catalog manager of a textile company in Canada, and as a columnist in several Canadian newspapers. In midlife, he went back to college at Eastern Mennonite University, then joined the staff of Mennonite Media Ministries, in Harrisonburg, Virginia. Even when he set up his own consulting agency, he continued to work for church and social agencies.

In 1989, Jim and his wife, Norma, broke the pattern of their lives to begin a two-year writing sabbatical in Nova Scotia. Jim and Norma are members of Blessed Sacrament Catholic Church in Harrisonburg. Jim is committed to the unity of the church. As a small gesture, he has never relinquished membership in the United Church of Canada, the Fellowship of Evangelical Baptists, and the Mennonite Church.

Fairfield holds a master of arts in religion from Eastern Mennonite Seminary. Jim was born in Manitoba and has dual citizenship, in Canada and in the USA. He attended the

University of Manitoba, where he met his wife. Their four children were born in Winnipeg, and their twelve grandchildren have been God's gifts to them in the United States.